SHAKESPEARE IN WARWICKSHIRE

→ SHAKESPEARE

in Warwickshire

Mark Williams Eccles,

THE UNIVERSITY OF WISCONSIN PRESS; MADISON, 1963

Published by The University of Wisconsin Press,
430 Sterling Court, Madison 6, Wisconsin

Copyright © 1961 by the Regents of the
University of Wisconsin

Paperback Edition, 1963

Printed in the United States of America

Library of Congress Catalog Card Number 61-5900

PREFACE

The picture of Shakespeare's life in Warwickshire is a mosaic with most of the pieces missing. Yet more records remain for Shakespeare than for most Elizabethan dramatists, and the archives of his native town tell a good deal about his father and about people he must have known, his friends and acquaintances. Here he grew up, his wife and children lived here, and in his last years he came home from London to Stratford. The men and women in his plays may owe something, now and then, to men and women in Stratford.

Shakespeare could not have written his plays if he had not lived at the heart of things, in London; but the plays would not have been what they are if he had been brought up in London, like Jonson and Middleton. He never forgot his roots in Stratford. It is hard to imagine Marlowe, if he had lived, retiring to Canterbury, or Greene to Norwich. Other playwrights spent some time in the counties of their birth, Beaumont in Leicestershire, Chapman in Hertfordshire, and Ford perhaps in Devonshire. Shakespeare, however, kept up an unusually close connection with the place where he was born. He chose to be known as William Shakespeare of Stratford upon Avon.

Until new discoveries are made about Shakespeare, we can only try to understand the little that is known. Most of the documents were found by Malone, Halliwell-Phillipps, and others, and are discussed in the masterly life by Sir Edmund Chambers. I have found no new records of Shakespeare, but I have examined the manuscript sources and have given my interpretation of the evidence. Special attention has been paid to friends and associates of Shakespeare, because knowledge of their lives may some day lead to more knowledge of Shakespeare.

Professor Allardyce Nicoll suggested this book and made me welcome as a visiting fellow of the Shakespeare Institute in Stratford. The writing was made possible by generous aid from the Fulbright Commission, the John Simon Guggenheim Memorial Foundation, and the Graduate School of the University of Wisconsin and by the hospitality of the Shakespeare Birthplace Library and the Folger Shakespeare Library. I have enjoyed exploring the lives of Shakespeare and his friends. I hope that readers will share some of my pleasure.

                                                            Mark Eccles

Madison, Wisconsin
April, 1960

CONTENTS

LIST OF ILLUSTRATIONS

SHAKESPEARE IN WARWICKSHIRE

CHAPTER I

THE SHAKESPEARES

AND THE ARDENS

❖Within the old forest of Arden, a few miles west of Kenilworth and twelve to fifteen miles north of Stratford, is a cluster
of four villages, Balsall, Baddesley Clinton, Wroxall, and Rowington. During the fourteenth and fifteenth centuries Balsall was
a commandery or estate of the Knights of St. John of Jerusalem;
Baddesley, one of the few places in England where a moat still
surrounds the great house, was the manor of James de Clinton and
his heirs; Wroxall belonged to the nuns of Wroxall Priory; and
Rowington was divided between Reading Abbey and Pinley Priory
in Rowington. In these villages, or in Coventry, lived all the
Shakespeares who have been found before 1500 in Warwickshire.
Shakespeare's grandfather, Richard, probably came from one of
these places to Snitterfield before 1529.[1]

We now know that at least one Shakespeare family in Stratford
descended from the Shakespeares of Balsall. In the reign of Richard II Adam and William Shakespere lived at Oldediche, in the
south part of Balsall bordering on Baddesley Clinton. William
Shakespere served on a coroner's jury at Balsall in 1385. According to a survey of the commandery made about 1538, Thomas
Shakespere then held a house and land in "Oldyche," as heir
of William Shakespere, by a copy of court roll granted to William
on the Monday after St. Andrew's day in some year (left blank)

in the reign of Richard II. In 1389 Adam Shakespere, "filius et
heres Adē de Oldediche," held lands on the manor of Baddesley
Clinton by military service. When he died in 1414 he left a widow
Alice and a minor son John, and John held the same lands in 1441.
The register of the gild of Knowle has two fifteenth-century entries
from Oldediche, for the souls of Richard and Alice Shakspere
about 1457 and for Robert Grene in 1498. Ralph Schakespeire and
his second wife joined the gild in 1464, and the next year Ralph
and Richard held Great Chedwyns in Baddesley, adjoining Wroxall.
Thomas Shakspere of Balsall and his wife Alice became members
of the gild in 1486, and their lands in "Oldiche" and elsewhere
in Balsall, granted by copy between 1485 and 1506, were held
about 1538 by their son and heir, the same Thomas who was also
heir of William. Thomas bought more land at Oldiche in 1540. A
John Shakeshaft, who was never called Shakespeare or identified
with Oldiche, appeared in many records at Balsall from 1536 to
1551, and a John Shakespeare hanged himself there in 1579.
Thomas Shaxpere of Warwick, shoemaker, who died in 1577, left
copyhold in Balsall to his wife Agnes for her life and named in his
will three sons, William, Thomas, and John. By the custom of the
manor the copyhold descended to the youngest son, John, a corviser
or shoemaker in Stratford. In 1596 John Shackspere of Stratford,
corviser, sold his copyhold of a house in Oldiche and of Dopkins
Orchard and other lands at Balsall, most of which had been held
about 1538 by Thomas, heir to the William Shakespere who was
living at Oldiche in the time of Richard II.[2]

Shakespeare's ancestors may have come from Balsall or they
may have come from Wroxall or Rowington. Elizabeth Shakspere
in 1417 forfeited copyhold on Wroxall manor. In 1464 Richard
Schakespeire of Wroxall and his wife Margery joined the gild of
Knowle. Isabel Shakspere was prioress of Wroxall Abbey in 1501
and Jane Shakspere was subprioress in 1525. One or more William
Shakesperes lived at Wroxall between 1504 and 1546 and at least
two Johns between 1507 and 1534. A John held land in Haseley
which in 1523 passed to Richard of Wroxall, who was bailiff of

Warwickshire

Wroxall manor in 1534. In Rowington, just south of Wroxall, John, Richard, and Thomas Shakespeare were recorded between 1460 and 1476. The Shakespeares in the four villages may have been related, since William Shakespere of Wroxall and John of Rowington were feoffees in 1504–5 for land which had belonged to Robert Hutsped of Hatton, whose wife Elizabeth had inherited from her father Ralph Shakspere land which had been held in 1389 by Adam Shakespere of Balsall and Baddesley Clinton. John Shakespere the elder and John the younger paid subsidy at Rowington in 1524–25. More Shakespeares lived in Rowington during the sixteenth century than in any other Warwickshire parish.[3]

Several early Shakespeares lived in the city of Coventry. Thomas Shakespere of Coventry, mercer, slew Robert Kyngton of Warwick, goldsmith, with his sword and fled in 1358. Richard Shakspere, wiredrawer, was killed there in 1416, Robert is named in the records of two Coventry gilds in 1485 and 1489, and another Richard received a bequest in 1500 from a Coventry merchant.[4]

Early in the sixteenth century Shakespeares began to appear elsewhere in Warwickshire. The nearest to Snitterfield was Richard Shakyspere of Hampton Corley in the parish of Budbrooke, near Warwick, who was on the subsidy roll for 1523. Some of the houses in Hampton Corley were owned by Wroxall Priory, according to the Valor Ecclesiasticus of 1535. Ralph Shakspere of Berkswell also paid subsidy in 1524–25. Richard Shakspere and his wife Margaret, living in 1539, but where is not known, were named in the will, proved at Stratford, of their son Thomas of Alcester, who paid subsidy for 1523, was bailiff of the manor in 1530, and left a young son William. Christopher Shakespere of Packwood, near Balsall, joined the gild of Knowle in 1511–12 with his wife Isabel and was a tenant at Packwood in 1544, with his sons William and John, and of chantry lands at Tanworth in 1553. He paid subsidy on ten pounds in goods in the second and third years of Edward VI. Richard Shakespeare held copyhold on Packwood manor in 1524 and 1540 and witnessed a deed there in 1555 with Christopher. The will of Christopher, made in 1557 and proved in 1558, named as executors his wife "Isbell" and his son Roger and as overseers his sons John and William and his son-in-law William Fetherstone. He left his dwelling house to Richard, evidently his eldest son, a copyhold house to William, and other bequests to his children Roger, Christopher, John, and Alice, who was also to have money which had been bequeathed to her by her brother Thomas. Each of the five sons surviving was to have "a cowe at the decease of my wyfe," and all but John had other legacies. One John Shakespeare of Stratford on Avon, yeoman, was named in a law-suit in Easter term, 1533; and in 1561 Roger Binford of Solihull sued for debt Richard Shackspere of Packwood, John Shackspere of Stratford on Avon, and Roger Shackspere of Packwood. These were probably the sons of Christopher, though it is possible that John was Shakespeare's father and a kinsman of the others. From a recusant list at Warwick Castle I find that a later Christopher Shackspere the elder and his wife were presented at Packwood in 1592 "for that they com not commonly to church." A John Shaxpere who witnessed a document at Lapworth in 1596 and bought property there in 1604 has been confused with Shakespeare's father, who died in 1601.[5]

Shakespeare's grandfather was in all probability Richard Shakespeare, a husbandman in Snitterfield from 1529 until his death in 1560 or early in 1561. He held land on two manors, one belonging to the collegiate church of St. Mary, Warwick, and then to the crown, the other to the crown and by 1560 to Bartholomew Hales and his wife Mary. The first record of any Shakespeare living at Snitterfield is on April 15, 1529, when Richard Shakkespere did not attend the manor court at Warwick, which was held by the deputy steward twice a year, at Hocktide after Easter and at Michaelmas, for the college tenants at Warwick and many other places besides Snitterfield. Rather than travel six miles to Warwick, he usually paid a fine of twopence, as many tenants did, though no fine was due when he sent a good excuse, as he did in 1532, 1538, and 1550. His name was copied as Richard "Shakstaff" in 1533, an entry which has been misread "Shakeschafte" and misdated in the thirty-third year of Henry VIII. Richard Shakkespere was ordered in 1538 to mend his hedges between his land and Thomas Palmer's.[6]

Richard also held land on the chief manor of Snitterfield, part of "Warwikeslands" which had belonged to the earls of Warwick. Records of this manor which were quoted by Halliwell-Phillipps and are now at the Birthplace Library include bailiff's accounts for 1438–39 and 1460–61, surveys made in 1545 and 1599, rentals of 1563 and 1581, and court rolls of 1507, 1535–43, and several years between 1560 and 1606. The survey of 1545 mentioned that Henry VIII had granted a fee as steward of the manor to Charles Brandon, Duke of Suffolk, and a fee as bailiff for life to Thomas, Lord Wriothesley (by a patent in 1530). No Shakespeare was named in 1507, but in 1535 the jury presented Richard Shakespere for overburdening the common pasture with his cattle, and the vicar, John Dune, for breaking the pound and taking out his animals. Richard was not one of the many who were fined for making frays, but on October 3, 1560, he was fined for not yoking or ringing his swine and for keeping his animals on the "leez" or meadows, and every tenant was ordered to "make his hedges & ditches betwixt the end of the lane of Richard Shakespere & the hedge called dawkins hedge." On October 1, 1561, after Richard had died and his holding was in his son's name, John Shakespere, Margery Lyncecombe, and William Rounde were each fined a shilling for not making their hedges according to the order. Richard Shakespeare had appraised the goods in 1559 of Roger Lyncecombe of Snitterfield and Henley Street, and Roger's widow Margery was living at Stratford in 1561, as was Shakespeare's father. John Shakespere probably sold his copyhold, since he does not appear in the next court rolls, for 1574 and later years.[7]

Adam Palmer testified in 1582 that Richard Shaxpere had lived in a house which was described in interrogatories as lying between the house formerly of William Palmer and Merrel Lane, "and doth abut on the High Street." Richard rented this house, with land reaching down to the brook that still flows through the village, from Robert Arden of Wilmcote, whose daughter Mary married Shakespeare's father.[8]

Richard Shakespere of Snitterfield was left "my foure oxen which are now in his keping" by the will in 1543 of Thomas Atwood alias Taylor of Stratford, a well-to-do alderman of the gild who named kinsmen at Rowington, Solihull, and Beoley. Richard witnessed the will of Henry Wager of Snitterfield in 1558 and helped to appraise the goods, valued at thirty-four pounds, of the vicar, Sir Thomas Hargreave, in 1557. He appraised the estates of three neighbors in 1559, and of three more in 1560, Thomas Palmer on January 3, Henry Cole, smith, on June 1, and Richard Maids on September 13. His own goods were valued at thirty-eight pounds seventeen shillings, but the inventory has not survived. He died before February 10, 1560/61, when administration of his estate was granted at Worcester to his son John, described in the bond as "Johannem Shakespere de Snytterfyld . . . agricolam." Shakespeare's father should have been described as of Stratford, glover, but the Worcester records make many errors. John's surety in giving a bond of a hundred pounds to the vicar general and the registrar of Bishop Sandys was Thomas Nycols of Snitterfield, husbandman, who witnessed a deed to Shakespeare's cousin Robert Webbe in 1576 and died in 1587. "John Shakespeare yeoman and Mary his wife" sold to Robert Webbe in 1579 their share of a house and cottage and a hundred acres of land in Snitterfield which had belonged to Robert Arden.[9]

Shakespeare had an uncle Henry in Snitterfield and possibly other uncles, though their relationship has not been established. Henry is called the brother of John of Stratford in a suit for debt in 1587. "Henry Shaxper" appraised the goods of John Pardie of Snitterfield in 1569/70. The will in 1573 of Alexander Webbe of Snitterfield, who had married Margaret Arden, names as an overseer "John Shackespere of Stretford upon Aven"; Henry was a witness and one of the appraisers with John. "Hary shakspere" was to be examined in 1582, with John Shakespeare, as a witness for Robert Webbe about the Arden property.[10]

Henry held land on the Hales manor in Snitterfield, where he was fined in 1574 for a fray on Edward Cornwell, who became Margaret Arden's second husband. In 1583 he was fined with two gentlemen and others for wearing a hat instead of a cap to church on Sundays and holidays and in 1596, shortly before his death, for not laboring with his team to mend the highways and "for having a diche betweene redd hill and Burman in decaye for want of repayringe." These fields can still be identified to the east of Snitterfield church.[11]

Henry "Saxspere" or "Shagspere" was involved in 1580 in a dispute over paying tithes on crops in Snitterfield. He testified at Worcester that he had paid tithe to Richard Brooke of Warwick, whom John Fisher charged with encouraging his followers to make frays and bloodshed in the fields of Snitterfield. Since Henry refused to pay his tithe again to other claimants, he was excommunicated until he would pay. He farmed land both at Snitterfield and at nearby Ingon in the parish of Hampton Lucy, where in 1570 John Shaxpere or his assigns occupied fourteen acres rented from William Clopton. Henry had two children christened at Hampton Lucy, Lettice in 1582 and James in 1585, but his son was buried in 1589 as "Jeames Shakespere of Yngon." In 1586 "Henry Shexsper" was one of the "pledges" or godparents for Henry Townsend at Snitterfield, and the will of Christopher Smith alias Court of Stratford mentioned that "Henry Shaxspere of Snytterfild" owed him five pounds. In the same year he borrowed twenty-two pounds from Nicholas Lane, who in 1587 sued John for ten pounds as surety for his brother Henry. He was imprisoned at Stratford in 1591 at the suit of Richard Ange in a plea of trespass on the case, and in September, 1596, was arrested for a debt to John Tomlins. While he was in prison for debt, his surety William Rounde went to his house and took away two oxen which Henry had bought but not yet paid for. Despite these debts, John Blythe declared that Henry died in his own house with money in his coffers and corn and hay in his barn "amounting to a great value." Henry Shakespeare was buried at Snitterfield on December

29, 1596, and his widow Margaret on February 9 following.[12]

The only other Shakespeare in the Snitterfield manor records is Thomas. He may have been another son of Richard, but proof is lacking. In 1563 "thomas shaxper" held copyhold at the largest rent on the Hales manor, four pounds; the only others who paid more than a pound were Edward Grant "for the scyte of the manor," the heirs of Thomas Cocke for freehold of "the farme ground," Thomas Stringer for two copyholds in Bearley, and Robert Nycols for a close on the demesne. He was chosen a tithingman in 1581, with Robert Webbe. Different stewards (Arthur Gregory and Henry Rogers) wrote his name on the homage or jury as "Shakesmore" in 1578, "shaxper" in 1581, and "Shackesper" in 1583. In 1581 he was fined for forestalling and engrossing barley, wheat, and rye, for overburdening the common, for not wearing a cap, and for not having and exercising bows and arrows; and in 1583 he was fined on the last two counts and for having unringed swine. All these were common charges, and he was on the jury in both years. He is not on the next surviving court rolls, from 1596 to 1606. His son John was christened at Snitterfield in 1581, but the names are too common to identify this boy with the John, "son to my brother Thomas," named in 1608 in the will of John Shakespeare of Clifford Chambers, Gloucestershire. A Thomas Shaxper witnessed in 1592 an attornment of tenants of the manors of Wolverton and Langley, next to Snitterfield, and Thomas Shakespeares lived at Warwick and at Rowington. Men of this name appeared in Stratford records between 1572 and 1586 and a "Thomas Green alias Shakspere" was buried there in 1589/90.[13]

Anthony Shaxpere of Snitterfield was a billman at the musters in 1569. A decidedly rolling stone, he married at Budbrooke in 1573, had a son Henry christened there in 1575 and buried at Clifford Chambers in 1583 and a daughter Elizabeth christened at Stratford in 1584, and was named in 1608 in the will of his brother John of Clifford Chambers. He married Joan Whetrefe, and a Joan Shaxspere died at Snitterfield in 1596. An Anthony

Shackspere was living at Balsall in 1602. "Wyllyam Shaxper" was named an overseer of the will of John Pardie of Snitterfield on December 25, 1569.[14]

Richard Shakespeare, then, seems to have been the father of John of Stratford, who was probably his eldest son, and of Henry, but not of Anthony. Thomas and William Shakespeare of Snitterfield may or may not have been other sons of Richard.

Shakespeare's mother was a daughter of Robert Arden of Wilmcote, husbandman, who was described in 1501 as son of Thomas Ardern of Wilmcote. Thomas may have been a grandson of Robert Arderne, bailiff of Snitterfield in 1438. There is no proof that Shakespeare was related to the Ardens of Park Hall, but it is possible that Thomas may have descended from a younger son of that family.

The Ardens of Park Hall were one of the few families in England who could trace their ancestors before the Conquest. Dugdale proved their descent from public records and from charters and deeds owned by Robert Arden, esquire (d. 1636). Alwin, sheriff of Warwick under Edward the Confessor, had a son Turchill of Warwick who called himself in 1088 "Turchillus de Eardene," Turchill of the forest of Arden. As Freeman wrote, "He stands out more conspicuously in Domesday than any other Englishman, his lands filling more than four columns." His manor of Curdworth was held by his son Siward de Arden and by his descendants until the attainder of Edward Arden of Park Hall in 1583.[15]

Park Hall, in Castle Bromwich in the parish of Aston near Birmingham, is first mentioned in 1364, and in 1373 Henry Arden secured release of all the services by which he held it, for the yearly payment of a red rose. He was knighted in 1375 and obtained other manors at red-rose rents from his liege lord Thomas de Beauchamp, Earl of Warwick. Though his younger sons, Geoffrey and William, died without heirs male, his eldest son, Sir Ralph, left a son Robert, eight years old at his father's death in 1420, when he became ward to Joan Beauchamp, Lady of Bergavenny. Robert was sheriff and knight of the shire, but for siding with the Duke of York he was executed as a traitor in 1452, leaving seven children. Four of these were sons, Walter, Thomas, John, and William.[16]

Walter Arden (1433–1502) recovered his father's lands and about 1457 joined the gild of Knowle with his wife Eleanor, daughter of John Hampden of Hampden. Park Hall descended to their son John, esquire of the body to Henry VII. By his will in 1502 "Water Arderne Esquire" left to Thomas, evidently his second son, ten marks a year for life, "whiche I have givin to him"; to his son Martin the manor of Nafford for life "yf it canne be recovered"; and if not, then to Martin and each of his other sons, Robert, Henry, and William, five marks a year for life. The will was witnessed by John Charnell and Thomas Arden, "Squiers," one a son-in-law and the other either the brother or the son of Walter. Thomas Ardern, "gentylman," sued his brother John in Chancery, between 1504 and 1515, for refusing to pay the annuity which his father had granted him out of Curdworth manor. Similar suits were brought against John by his mother Eleanor and in 1524 by his brother Henry. In 1526 Martin and Robert Ardern witnessed the will of Sir John, who confirmed their annuities by declaring, "I will that my brothers Thomas, Martin & Robert have their fees during their lives." Thomas became bailiff of the castle and manor of Codnor, Derbyshire, and his bond to the king for this office was given on August 25, 1501, by John Ardren, esquire, Robert Ardren, gent., and Roger Wood, merchant of Coventry. Robert Ardern, groom of the chamber, had a patent for the same office on September 19, 1501. Either Sir John's brother or his son Thomas (1486–1563) may have been the Thomas Ardern of Warwickshire listed in 1525/6 among "Sewers of the Chamber, out of wages," or no longer regularly at court. A Thomas Arden, gentleman, was a juror in 1525 at Warwick for the inquisition post mortem of Sir Thomas Lucy. Martin Arden was farmer and bailiff of royal manors in Staffordshire before 1506. Robert in 1502 was groom of the chamber, keeper of two royal parks, and escheator for Nottingham and Derby, and in 1509 he was described as Robert Ardren of Holme in Nottinghamshire, "Goodenor" (Codnor) in Derbyshire, Rowley and Yoxall in Staffordshire, esquire or gentleman, and sewer of the king's chamber. He was an esquire in 1526, when he had an annuity from the manor of Warde Barnes near "Wilemcote" (Wilnecote in Tamworth). Henry, also a groom of the chamber, was described in 1509 as of Aston and Kenilworth in Warwickshire and of Stratton in the parish of Biggleswade, Bedfordshire. Henry Ardern, of Hadley, Middlesex, sued his brother John Ardern, esquire, in 1524 for destroying the seal of the deed giving Henry his annuity from Park Hall and other lands in Warwickshire and Worcestershire. William may have died before 1512, when payment was made to the gild of Knowle by Alice Arderne for herself and for the soul of William. No connection has so far been found between the Ardens or Arderns of Park Hall and Thomas Ardern of Wilmcote.[17]

Halliwell-Phillipps suggested that Robert Arden, Shakespeare's grandfather, "was most likely the grandson of a Robert Ardern who was the bailiff of Snitterfield about the middle of the fifteenth century, and who is also mentioned in a record of 1461 as *nuper firmarius terre dominice ibidem*." These records are now in the Birthplace Library: the account for 1438–39 of Robert Arderne, bailiff of the Earl of Warwick's manor in Snitterfield, and the account for 1460–61 of John Buxston, bailiff, which mentions as still living Robert Arderne, lately farmer of the demesne land there. Robert Arderne of Snitterfield and his wife joined the gild of Stratford in 1440–41 and he served on coroner's juries in 1443–44. There were other Ardens in Warwickshire, for John Aredene of Long Itchington joined the gild of Knowle soon after 1460, and his son Richard in 1504, and in 1506 payment was made for the soul of John Ardernne of Marton. Geoffrey Ardern was sheriff of Coventry in 1478 and Robert Ardern, fellow of Merton College, Oxford, became rector of Lapworth in 1489. But Robert Arderne of Snitterfield is the only fifteenth-century Arden who is known to have lived near Stratford. He may have been the grandfather, not of Robert Arden, but of Thomas Ardern of Wilmcote.[18]

Mary Arden's grandfather, Thomas Ardern of Wilmcote, bought property in Snitterfield on May 10, 1501, when John Mayowe made a deed to Robert Throkmerton, esquire, Thomas Trussell of Billesley, Roger Reynolds of Henley in Arden, William Wodde of Wodhouse, Thomas Ardern of Wilmcote, and Robert Ardern, son of the same Thomas. The property was described as a house between land of John Palmer and a lane called "Merellane" in breadth, and in length from the king's highway to a certain brook, with all the lands belonging to it in the town and fields of Snitterfield. Mayowe's attorneys to deliver seisin were Thomas Clopton, gentleman, and John Porter, both of Snitterfield. John, son and heir of Richard Mayowe, secured a grant or release of this property from William Mayowe in 1503. In a second deed made on July 6, 1504, by John "Mayhow" to Thomas "Arthurn" of Wilmcote, the same property was described as a house between the tenement of William Palmer and "Maryes lane," with eighty acres of land. Of the four men named in trust in 1501, Robert Throckmorton of Coughton, knighted in November, 1501, was a trustee for Walter Arden of Park Hall in a settlement on his wife Eleanor and for John Arden of Park Hall in another deed before 1510. He made his will in 1518 and died on a pilgrimage to Jerusalem. His inquisition post mortem shows that he held lands and tenements in Snitterfield. Thomas Trussell should also have been described as "esquire," as he was in a deed of 1489 and in a document of 1509. He was chosen sheriff in 1507 and died in 1517. Roger Reynolds died before 1507, when his father, William of Henley, made Sir Robert Throckmorton an overseer of his will and guardian of his grandson William and left a bequest to the gild of Aston Cantlow from "my land there called Pathlowe." William Wood lived in Great Alne, where his family was called "de Bosco" in 1236 and "Atte Wode" in 1334, and their manor of Woodhouse was held by feoffees for the late Thomas Atte Wode in 1482 and by Thomas Atwood, who died in

1521. In the time of Charles I Edward Atwood described in Chancery the custom of the manor of Aston Cantlow, by which the eldest son inherited copyhold.[19]

In the subsidy for 1523 Thomas Arden of Aston Cantlow was assessed on goods valued at twelve pounds. He owed suit to Warwick College for his land at Snitterfield in 1525 and probably died soon afterward, for no later court roll mentions him. He may have had a younger son named Thomas, since in the subsidy for 1546 a Thomas Arden of Aston Cantlow was assessed on only two pounds a year in land, and a Thomas Arden, not resident in Stratford, held property in the town in 1560. A Christopher Ardern was buried in 1581 at Aston Cantlow and an Elizabeth Arden in 1588.[20]

John Henley, aged eighty, testified in 1582 that he had known since about 1516 the freehold in Snitterfield of Thomas Arden and his son Robert. Robert bought a second freehold there from the daughters of William Harvey and their husbands, part from Richard and Agnes Rushby in 1519 and part from John and Elizabeth Palmer in 1529. For each of his two freeholds on the Warwick College manor he paid in 1546 a chief rent of four shillings and a cock and two hens. In 1533 he was ordered to mend his hedges between his land and John Palmer's, and in that year and in 1538 he was fined for not attending the manor court at Warwick.[21]

Robert Arden became a brother of the Stratford gild in 1517–18 and in the same year, as "Robert Arthern," of the gild of Knowle. Probably he also belonged to the gild of his own parish, Aston Cantlow, where no records remain. He was assessed there in 1523 on eight pounds in goods and in 1546 on ten pounds a year in land. In 1549 he witnessed the will of Richard Green of Great Wilmcote, and in 1553 he sued John Dyckson for debt in the Stratford court of record. By his first wife, or possibly more than one, he had eight daughters. When he was fifty or more he married again, for on April 21, 1548, Agnes Hill, widow, secured license from the steward of Balsall manor to marry Robert Ardern. Both she and Robert held land from Balsall manor, which be-

longed to the Knights of St. John of Jerusalem and then to Queen
Katherine Parr. Her first husband, John Hill of Bearley, who
leased Bearley manor or grange from Bordesley Abbey, had died
in 1545, leaving her with four young children, John, Eleanor,
Mary, and Thomas.[22]

Where the Ardens lived in Wilmcote is not known. An inventor
of legends, John Jordan, claimed in 1794 that they had occupied
a house in Featherbed Lane, now called "Mary Arden's House."
Thomas Finderne of Nuneaton sold this house in 1561, with the
manor of Great Wilmcote, to Adam Palmer and George Gibbes.
The house has oak beams of the early sixteenth century, a large
stone dovecot, and a cider mill and farming gear assembled by
the Birthplace trustees, who bought the property in 1930. It gives
an excellent idea of the kind of farmhouse in which Shakespeare's mother grew up.[23]

On July 17, 1550, Robert Ardern, "husbandman," conveyed
his house and land in Snitterfield in the tenure of Richard Shakespere to trustees, Adam Palmer and Hugh Porter, for the use of
himself and his wife Agnes during their lives, and then to be divided among three of his daughters: Agnes wife of Thomas
Stringer, Joan wife of Edmund Lambert, and Katherine wife of
Thomas "Etkyns" or Edkins of Wilmcote. A like deed on the
same day conveyed the former Harvey freehold, including a house
in the tenure of Richard Henley and a cottage in the tenure of
Hugh Porter, to be divided eventually among three other daughters: Margaret wife of Alexander Webbe of Bearley, Joyce Ardern,
and Alice Ardern. Elizabeth and Mary, not named in these deeds,
later inherited a sixth share each in the shares of their sisters Joyce
and Alice.[24]

Making his will on November 24, 1556, Robert Arden of
Wilmcote left "to my youngste dowghter Marye all my lande in
Willmecote cawlide Asbyes and the crop apone the grounde
sowne and tyllide as hitt is," with ten marks in money. He gave
Alice the third part of his goods "in fylde and towne" and named
Alice and Mary executors. "Annes my wife" was to have ten

marks on condition that she should suffer Alice quietly to enjoy half the copyhold in Wilmcote; if not, then only five marks and her "gintur" (jointure) in Snitterfield. The overseers, Adam Palmer, Hugh Porter, and John Skerlett, were to divide the rest of his goods equally among his other children. His goods were valued, on December 9, at £77 11s. 10d. and his will was proved at Worcester on December 16. The inventory includes painted cloths in the hall and chamber, oxen, bullocks, kine, "wayning caves," horses, sheep, swine, bees and poultry, "and the baken in the roffe." The will was witnessed by several neighbors and by "Sir Wylliam Borton, curett," who became vicar of Snitterfield the next year but was replaced in 1561 for refusing to take the oath of supremacy. Robert bequeathed his soul in Catholic terms, "to Allmyghtye God and to our bleside Laydye Sent Marye, and to all the holye companye of heven." He wished to be buried in the churchyard of St. John the Baptist in Aston Cantlow, but he made no bequests to churches as did Christopher Shakespeare of Packwood in 1557 or Henry Cole of Snitterfield in 1560.[25]

Robert's widow Agnes remained at Wilmcote and was buried at Aston Cantlow on December 29, 1580. In 1560 she leased the two freeholds in Snitterfield to her brother Alexander Webbe, with rights of "housebote, ploughbote, cartbote, and hedgebote." On July 5, 1580, she made an affidavit declaring that she would testify in a Chancery suit "if I weare able to travell being aged and impotent," and Bartholomew Hales and Nicholas Knolles were therefore named on November 25 to take her testimony at home as a defendant to Thomas Mayowe. Her will left gifts to her godchildren, to Alexander Webbe's children, and to Joan Lambert, and most of her goods, which were valued at forty-five pounds, to her son John Hill and her son-in-law John Fulwood for the benefit of her grandchildren. The executors were Hill and Fulwood, the overseers Adam Palmer and George Gibbes.[26]

Shakespeare had many first cousins on his mother's side. Her sister Agnes was twice married: first to John Hewyns of Bearley, and second to Thomas Stringer, as Robert Arden mentioned in

July, 1550. The Bearley register dates the marriage of Stringer to Agnes "Hwens" (*sic*) October 15, 1550, but the register is a transcript made in 1598 and it makes another mistake in dating the christening of Alice, daughter to Thomas Stringer, on July 10, and her burial on June 10, both in 1552. Thomas Stringer's son John was christened on May 20, 1554, and his son "Areden" on February 24, 1555/6. Thomas appears from 1560 to 1583 on the court rolls of the Hales manor in Snitterfield, where in 1561 he and his son "Arderne" had license to lease copyhold in Bearley, and in 1563 he held a house and two yardlands in Bearley and one yardland "sumtyme in the tennur of hewyns." In 1575 he held freehold in Snitterfield and was described in a court roll as resident on the manor, but he was called Thomas Stringer of Stockton, Shropshire, yeoman, in a lease and a bond of 1568/9, both made in the presence of "John Shaxpere," and again in 1576 and 1578 when he, with his sons John and Arden, sold all their rights to the inheritance of his late wife Agnes. Agnes had evidently died before 1569.[27]

Joan Arden had married by 1550 Edmund Lambert of Barton on the Heath, fifteen miles south of Stratford. Shakespeare may have been thinking of this village when he called Christopher Sly "old Sly's son of Burton Heath." John and Mary Shakespeare mortgaged one of their Wilmcote estates in 1578 to Edmund Lambert, yeoman. "Jhohan Lamberde" was mentioned in the will of her stepmother and she and Edmund were defendants to Thomas Mayowe in 1582, although they had sold their share in the Arden estate to Robert Webbe in 1581. "Edmund Lambarte, senior" was buried at Barton on April 23, 1587, and "Joanna Lambarte, vidua" on November 30, 1593. Shakespeare's father sued their son John, calling him a man of great wealth and well friended. Edmund Lambert was probably godfather to Edmund Shakespeare in 1580 and Joan probably godmother to the two Joan Shakespeares in 1558 and 1569.[28]

Katherine Arden was the wife in 1550 of Thomas "Etkyns" or Edkins of Wilmcote. She and her husband sold their reversion to

Thomas Stringer and on October 16, 1576, promised to sue forth at the next term, in January, a fine which they had acknowledged, if Katherine should live so long. She had died by 1578, when only Thomas Edkins was named. Thomas Edkins the elder and Thomas the younger appraised the goods of Agnes Arden in 1581 and both owned grain in 1595, when Adam Edkins was bound for Thomas the elder.[29]

Elizabeth Arden married a Scarlett or Skarlett, whose first name is not known, and died before March 18, 1581/2, when John Skarlett of Newnham in the parish of Aston Cantlow, husbandman, son and heir of Elizabeth Skarlett, daughter and coheir of Robert Arden, sold his share of land in Snitterfield to Robert Webbe. John had then a wife Joan, and in 1595 a John Scarlet had a household of fourteen persons at Aston Cantlow. An earlier John Skarlett, named in the subsidy of 1546, was witness and overseer of Robert Arden's will in 1556; another Joan, wife of John Scarlett, was buried at Aston Cantlow in 1580 and John Scarlett in 1581; and the will of John Scarlett of Newnham in 1581 mentioned a brother William and a John, son of Adam Scarlett. Adam Scarlett of Wilmcote died in 1591, the richest yeoman in the parish.[30]

Margaret Arden lived until 1614, longer than any of her sisters. She was probably godmother to Margaret Shakespeare in 1562. By 1550 she had married Alexander Webbe of Bearley, called "Saunder Webbe" by Adam Palmer and "elyxaunder web of bereley" when Ralph Cawdrey assaulted him in 1559. In May, 1560, he leased from his sister Agnes Arden, widow, for her life or forty years to begin on March 25, 1561, the two houses with a cottage and land in Snitterfield occupied by Richard Shakespere, John Henley, and John Hargreve. He lived in the Shakespere house after Richard's death, though he also leased land in Bearley from Adrian Quiney in September, 1560. His son Edward was christened at Snitterfield on July 30, 1562, and his daughter Sara on April 23, 1565, and Alexander was buried there on April 17, 1573. The will of Alexander Webbe of Snitterfield, husbandman, made his wife Margaret executrix, asking her to "see my children vertusly brought up," and left legacies to their six children, Robert, Edward, Anne, Elizabeth, Mary, and Sara. John Shakespere of Stratford and John Hill of Bearley were overseers of his will and appraisers of his goods, valued at forty pounds.[31]

Margaret Webbe married a second husband, Edward Cornwell, before 1574/5, when they held freehold in Snitterfield. Cornwell was constable in 1574, when Henry Shakespere assaulted him, and in 1578, when Edward Grant, gentleman, assaulted him twice, once with a dagger and once with a staff. He was fined for frays with John Tomes in 1581 and 1583. Edward and Margaret bought a reversion in 1576 from Thomas Stringer and sold their shares to Robert Webbe, who in 1578 also bought all Edward's goods except a bay mare and one coffer. He was probably the "Cornishe" named in a will of 1578 as surety with Edmund Lambert for the debt of John Shakespeare, and he witnessed deeds by Lambert in 1581. He leased a house and orchard to William Perkes, promising to pay him five marks a year if he were put out of possession by the "heires of the Ardens." Edward appears on court rolls of 1602 and 1603. After "Margareta uxor Edwardi Cornehill' was buried on August 26, 1614, he married again, for he had a son Edward christened in 1620 and a daughter Mary in 1621, but "Edwardus Cornell" was buried on March 4, 1623/4.[32]

Robert Webbe left more records than any other of Shakespeare's cousins. He bought from his mother and stepfather in 1576 their lease from Agnes Arden and their share in the estate after the death of Agnes, and in 1578 the shares which they had bought from the Stringers and Thomas Edkins. He secured the share of John and Mary Shakespeare in 1579 for four pounds (probably not forty pounds, as the fine gave it, since this was not a full share); the share of Edmund and Joan Lambert in 1581 for forty pounds; and the share of John Skarlett in 1581/2 for twenty marks. Thomas Mayowe brought a Chancery suit against Edward Cornwell, Agnes Arden, and Robert Webbe, claiming by entail the property sold by John Mayowe in 1501 and 1504. Agnes Arden made her affidavit in this case in 1580. John Shakespeare was subpenaed as a witness in May, 1582, but his deposition has not been found. Adam Palmer, John Henley, and John Wager testified in June, 1582, that the fee simple belonged to Thomas and Robert Arden and now to Robert Webbe. In consideration of his coming marriage to Mary Perkes, and for thirty-five pounds, Robert Webbe on September 1, 1581, leased two houses for six years to her father John, and John agreed to find "meate drincke chamber lodging & fier" in his house for Robert and Mary and any children they might have and for Robert's mother and her husband Edward "Cornell," Edward to pay three pounds a year "for his bording" and Robert to grant "sufficient hedgboot and fierboot." Robert and Mary Webbe had seven children, most of them given Biblical names: Hester or Esther, William, Martha, Mary, Elias, Prudence, and John. The leet presented Robert in 1583 as a common player at bowls and in 1596 for not wearing a cap. When he died in 1597, his goods were valued at fifty-one pounds by William Meads and Edward Cornwell.[33]

Joyce Arden is mentioned only in the deed of Robert Arden in 1550 which settled a freehold in Snitterfield upon his daughters Margaret Webbe, Joyce Arden, and Alice Arden. By his will in 1556 Alice was also to have a third of his goods and half his copyhold in Wilmcote. Joyce and Alice probably died unmarried, for their six sisters inherited their reversionary rights in the Snitterfield estate.

Mary, the youngest daughter of Robert Arden, proved his will, with Alice, in December, 1556. Soon after, she married John Shakespeare. She must have been born within a few years of 1540, since her children were born from 1558 to 1580. When she died in 1608, either in Henley Street or at New Place, she was survived by four of her eight children, William, Gilbert, Joan, and Richard; by four grandchildren, Susanna Hall, Judith Shakespeare, William Hart, and Thomas Hart; and by one great-grandchild, Elizabeth Hall.

Shakespeare's grandfathers were both plain countrymen, Richard

Shakespeare, husbandman, and Robert Arden, husbandman. Though the Ardens may have descended from an ancient family, there is no record that Robert Arden or his father Thomas claimed the title of gentleman. If John Shakespeare had remained on the land, Shakespeare might, like his forefathers, have followed the ever-running year with profitable labor to his grave. But John Shakespeare came to Stratford and William had his chance to go to school.

CHAPTER II

SHAKESPEARE'S

FATHER

❖Since John Shakespeare was a householder in Stratford by 1552, he was probably born before 1530. He learned the mystery of a glover and whittawer, which required an apprenticeship of at least seven years. One glover who might have been his master was Thomas Dickson alias Waterman of Bridge Street (alderman in 1553, d. 1557), whose wife was Joan, daughter of John Townsend of the Wold in Snitterfield. Glovers flourished in Stratford at this time and on market and fair days had the chief standing in the town, at the High Cross. Though they had no formal company before 1606, they probably observed some of the customs approved in 1637, which mentioned sheepskins, lambskins, and calfskins and provided that only an apprentice or master might sell "gloves purses or other wares belonging to the trade."[1]

At the court leet for the king's manor of Stratford held on April 29, 1552, John Shakyspere was fined for making a muckhill in Henley Street. Others were fined for the like offense, including Adrian Quiney and Richard Symons, deputy steward of the manor. In 1556 John Shakespere bought from Edward West a house and garden in Henley Street and from George Turnor a house with garden and croft (enclosed land) in Greenhill Street. An earlier George Turnour had bought in 1502, for a hundred silver marks, eight houses, four tofts (plots of ground), and four acres of land in Stratford, perhaps including the house in Greenhill Street. John Shakespeare sold this house before 1590, when the only houses he owned in Stratford were two in Henley Street. It is fortunate that his purchases in 1556 happen to be recorded, for the few surviving court rolls of the borough mention only three other purchases, all in 1556 or 1557.[2]

John Shakyspere, glover, was sued in 1556 for eight pounds by Thomas Siche of "arscotte," Worcestershire, called Thomas Such of Armscote, husbandman, in his will, proved the next year. John defended the action and won his case. In September he was chosen a taster to inspect ale and bread, and in November he was named an arbiter in one suit and brought another against Henry Field for eighteen quarters of barley. John Shakespeare was often plaintiff or defendant in the court of record, usually for debt or trespass, and he was again chosen to arbitrate suits in 1559 and 1569. It is possible that some of these suits may refer to another John, such as the John Shackspere of Stratford who was sued in 1561 with Richard and Roger Shackspere of Packwood; and many later suits clearly involved the corviser, who is first heard of at Stratford in 1584. John of Clifford Chambers, who married in 1560 and died in 1610, sued William Smith of Stratford for debt in 1572 and owed money in 1583 to John Ashwell of Stratford, one of the men sued by a John Shakespere in 1557.[3]

The marriage of Shakespeare's father to Mary Arden probably took place in 1557 at Aston Cantlow. She was unmarried on November 24, 1556, when Robert Arden left her ten marks and land in Wilmcote. Her first child, Joan, was christened on September 15, 1558. Wooing and wedding made 1557 a busy year for John, and he was fined in June for not having attended as a taster at three sessions of the court of record, which met once a fortnight. His name was crossed out as a juror at the leet on April 30, but he served on October 1 and brought three lawsuits in September and October. In April, 1559, he was fined, with others including the bailiff and Master Clopton of New Place, "for not kepynge ther gutteres cleane." He was chosen one of the four constables in

1558 and 1559, and in 1559 and 1561 he witnessed the minutes of the leet as one of the affeerors, who assessed fines. Instead of signing his name he made his mark, a pair of glover's compasses. The same mark appears in 1564 and a different mark in 1563. Since he grew up in a country village, he had not had a chance to attend school; and like most of his generation, he never found it necessary to learn to write.[4]

From 1561 to 1563 John Shakespeare and John Taylor were the two chamberlains, who had charge of borough property and finances. As was customary, their official accounts were drawn up by the deputy steward, Richard Symons. John Shakespeare did more than his share of this work, for the accounts of the next chamberlains, William Tyler and William Smith, were in 1564/5 "made by John Shakspeyr & John tayler" and in 1565/6 "made by John Shakspeyr." No one else looked after town business for so many years. At some time before he became chamberlain, he had been chosen one of the chief burgesses, or members of the town council. In the plague year of 1564 he was one of the burgesses who in August attended a council meeting in the chapel garden, to avoid infection, and contributed to relieve the poor.[5]

The Shakespeares' second child, Margaret, was christened on December 2, 1562, and buried on April 30, 1563. William, their first son, was christened on April 26, 1564, and Gilbert, their second, on October 13, 1566. Gilbert may have been named for Gilbert Bradley, a glover in Henley Street who became a burgess in 1565. Malone suggested that William might have been named for William Smith, haberdasher, of Henley Street, for whom John was acting as chamberlain, but the name is too common to justify guessing at godfathers. Fortunately the boy escaped the plague which struck Stratford in July, 1564, when the register noted "Hic incepit pestis," and which took four children of Roger Green in Henley Street. William's sister Joan had probably died in 1559 or 1560, when few burials were recorded. John and Mary Shakespeare had four more children: a second Joan, christened on April 15, 1569; Anne, christened on September 28, 1571, and buried on April 4,

1579, with a special fee for "the bell & paull"; Richard, christened on March 11, 1573/4; and Edmund, on May 3, 1580.[6]

John Shakespeare was elected one of the fourteen aldermen on July 4, 1565, to replace William Bott of New Place, who had been expelled in May. After he was sworn on September 12, he was entitled to wear in public a gown of black cloth faced with fur. He was taxed in the subsidy book in 1567 on an assessment set in one record at three pounds and in another at four pounds in goods. After being one of three nominees in 1567, he was chosen bailiff or chief officer of Stratford in 1568, taking office on October first. He presided at council meetings in the gild hall and at sessions of the court of record as a justice of peace during his year of office. Professional players first acted in Stratford about August, 1569, while he was bailiff: the Queen's players, who were rewarded with nine shillings, and the Earl of Worcester's men, who were given only one shilling. In 1571 he was chosen chief alderman, serving as a justice of peace and as deputy to the new bailiff, Adrian Quiney. The next January the two men were instructed to go to London for Hilary term and to deal in the affairs of the borough according to their discretions. John sued in the court of Common Pleas at Westminster in 1572 and recovered a debt of fifty pounds from John Luther of Banbury, glover, one of the original aldermen of that town. In the same court Mr. Henry Higford of Solihull, who had been steward of Stratford from 1566 to 1570, sued John Shakysper of Stratford, "whyttawer," for a debt of thirty pounds in 1573 and again in 1578. John became tenant of Ingon Meadow between 1568 and 1570, when William Clopton sold it with other lands to Rice Griffin, and in 1575 he paid ten pounds for a better lease of the fourteen acres called "Over Yngon medowe alias Yngon medowe."[7]

By a final agreement recorded at Westminster in October, 1575, John Shakespere bought two houses in Stratford, with gardens and orchards, for forty pounds, from Edmund and Emma Hall of Hallow in the parish of Grimley, near Worcester. There is nothing to show that either of these houses was in Henley Street. He leased a house in Stratford to William Burbage, but in July, 1582, arbiters agreed that John should release William from the bargain and repay seven pounds of the amount he had received. Burbage was still trying to collect this money in 1592.[8]

Shakespeare's father seems to have considered applying for a grant of arms at some time after he became bailiff, since a herald wrote in 1596 that he showed a pattern of arms attested by Robert Cook, Clarencieux herald, "xx years past," though this date is only approximate. Lack of money may have led to the delay. John Shakespeare bought no more houses or land after 1575. He attended every council meeting for which attendance is recorded from his election as bailiff through 1576, but he was absent from every later meeting for which attendance is recorded except one on September 5, 1582. His brother aldermen in January, 1577/8, reduced his tax for equipping soldiers from the amount assessed on an alderman to the amount assessed on a burgess, and this tax remained unpaid a year later. They did not fine him for his absence on election day in September, 1578, as they did John Wheeler, and in November they ordered "that euery alderman shall paye weekely towardes the releif of the poore iiij^d savinge m^r John shaxpeare and m^r Robert bratt who shall not be taxed to paye any thinge." Bratt had retired as alderman by 1570. John Shakespeare remained an alderman for nearly ten years after he last attended regularly, but finally in September, 1586, two new aldermen were chosen "for that m^r wheler dothe desyre to be put out of the Companye & m^r Shaxspere dothe not Come to the halles when they be warned nor hathe not done of Longe tyme." No other alderman was allowed to hold office so long without attending meetings. Both he and his brother aldermen may have hoped, year by year, that his clouded fortunes would shine again.[9]

John Shakespeare borrowed forty pounds by mortgaging on November 14, 1578, a house and fifty-six acres in Wilmcote, part of his wife's inheritance, to her sister's husband Edmund Lambert of Barton Henmarsh or Barton on the Heath. He was already in debt to Lambert, and on the same day as the mortgage Roger Sadler mentioned in his will that Edmund Lambert and "Cornishe" (Edward Cornwell) owed him five pounds for the debt of John Shakespeare. Since John did not repay Lambert the forty pounds when it came due at Michaelmas, 1580, Edmund remained owner of the Wilmcote property till his death in 1587, though a lease made by the Shakespeares was still in force in 1597. John sued Edmund's son and heir John Lambert in the court of Queen's Bench at Westminster in Michaelmas term, 1588. He declared that at Stratford on September 26, 1587, John Lambert had promised to pay twenty pounds more in return for full assurance of title by John and Mary Shakespeare and their son William and delivery of the evidences. Lambert denied making this promise. In November, 1597, John and Mary Shakespeare sued in Chancery, declaring that John Shakespeare had offered the forty pounds but that Edmund had refused it and had said the Shakespeares should not have the property unless they paid him other money which they owed him. John Lambert answered that John Shakespeare had mortgaged the property by indenture, confirmed "by his Deede Pole and Liverie" and by fine in Queen's Bench; that he had not tendered or paid the money at the date when it was due; and that the suits were intended "to wringe from him this defendante some further recompence," since the lease was "nowe somewhat nere expyred, wherby a greater value is to be yearly raised therby." His counsel Mr. Overbury, the father of Sir Thomas, protested in 1599 that John Shakespeare had brought a second Chancery bill in his own name only on the same matter. Two men chosen by John Shakespeare, Richard Lane and John Combe, and two others chosen by Lambert were ordered to examine witnesses, but the depositions, though they were taken, have not been found. John Shakespeare never recovered the property. I have discovered a hitherto unnoticed fine recorded in Easter term, 1602, which shows that John Lambert and Margery his wife sold to Richard Smyth, for forty pounds, forty-six acres of land in Great Wilmcote, together with two acres of meadow, three acres of pasture, and common of pasture.[10]

Robert Arden had left to his daughter Mary "my lande in Willmecote cawlid Asbyes." This name does not appear again in the records, but either Asbyes or the land mortgaged to Lambert may have included a "close of John Shakesperes" mentioned as next to "the Meadow-Piece adjoining to Shelfyll" in 1575, when Adam Palmer and George Gibbes divided their manor of Great Wilmcote. By an agreement made on November 12, 1578, John and Mary Shakespeare and George Gibbes conveyed eighty-six acres in Wilmcote, including six of meadow and ten of pasture, to Thomas Webbe and Humphrey Hooper, who in return granted a lease to George Gibbes for twenty-one years from Michaelmas, 1580. At Michaelmas, 1601, the land was to revert to John and Mary Shakespeare for Mary's heirs. Although this transaction has been called mysterious, a possible explanation can be suggested. Gibbes, who probably held the land by lease, secured a new lease and had it put on record in Queen's Bench by means of a fine to Webbe and Hooper, acting as trustees. Since the fine names no purchase price, the Shakespeares were not selling or mortgaging this land, but Gibbes probably made the usual payment for a new lease. He agreed to pay Webbe and Hooper a nominal rent, four bushels of wheat and four of barley every Christmas. John and Mary Shakespeare, or her heirs, may have sold Asbyes later, but no further record has been found. The advantage of the bargain for John Shakespeare was that it brought in ready money, like the mortgage to Lambert.[11]

John and Mary Shakespeare also had a ninth share (a sixth part of two thirds), because of the deaths of her sisters Joyce and Alice, in two houses and a hundred acres at Snitterfield which had been leased to Alexander Webbe. This share they sold to his son Robert Webbe on October 15, 1579, for four pounds (probably not forty pounds, as recorded in the fine of 1580). John and Mary signed by mark an indenture and a bond, in the presence of Nicholas Knooles or Knolles, vicar of Alveston, Anthony Osbaston, and William Maydes or Meades (a neighbor of Henry Shakespeare). John's seal on the bond has "I S" and Mary's has a running horse.[12]

John Shakespeare of Stratford, yeoman, was fined twenty pounds in Trinity term, 1580, for not appearing in Queen's Bench to find surety for keeping the peace towards the queen and all her people, and twenty pounds more as pledge for John Audeley of the town of Nottingham, hatmaker, who had not appeared to find surety for good behavior. Audeley was fined forty pounds on this charge, twenty more for not finding surety to keep the peace, and ten more as pledge for Shakespeare, and Thomas Cooley of Stoke, Staffordshire, was fined twenty as pledge for Audeley and ten as pledge for Shakespeare. The court reported these fines to the Exchequer for collection, though there is no record that they were paid. The reason for requiring sureties is not known, but more than a hundred and forty men throughout England were fined at the same time by the crown.[13]

Shakespeare's father had also private enemies, for in Trinity term (June 15–July 4), 1582, he petitioned the court of Queen's Bench for sureties of the peace against Ralph Cawdrey, William Russell, Thomas Logginge, and Robert Young, "for fear of death and mutilation of his limbs." Alderman Cawdrey, a butcher in Bridge Street since 1541, was then bailiff of Stratford, but in 1559 he had been fined "for makynge afray uppon elyxaunder web of bereley," John Shakespeare's brother-in-law, and in 1560 for an affray upon Grene of Wootton. Robert Young, dyer, married Margaret Field in 1586 and died in 1595. He gave surety in 1587 for John Shaxpere, shoemaker, and John Shaxpere sued him in 1591, when Sir Thomas Lucy also sued him on a bond. Ursula Field, his mother-in-law, had Young and William Sampson bound to keep the peace in 1590, and Young in turn had the bailiff bind Ursula to keep the peace. Alderman Shakespeare, who had not been recorded as present at a council meeting since 1576, attended on September 5, 1582, and voted for John Sadler, who was chosen bailiff. Since Cawdrey also attended, the two neighbors were probably reconciled.[14]

Another John Shakespeare, a corviser or shoemaker from Warwick, married at Stratford in 1584 Margery, widow of Thomas Roberts, shoemaker, and lived in a house in Bridge Street which

Roberts had leased. After his wife died in 1587, he married again and had three children at Stratford, Ursula, Humphrey, and Philip. He served as taster in 1585, as constable the next two years, and as master of his company in 1592. This man may have been the John Shackspere who was sued for debt by John Browne in October, 1585, and was ordered arrested for the debt in January and March, 1585/6. One of the two Johns was a juror in the court of record in May and July, 1586, in 1590, and in 1591. Although Shakespeare's father had brought many suits in this court before he became alderman, the incomplete register shows none while he was alderman from 1565 to 1586. Suits from 1588 to 1595 may all refer to the shoemaker. Seven suits were brought by a John Shakespeare between 1588 and 1591; Richard Tyler sued John Shaksper, shoemaker, for debt in 1591 and a John Shaxpere in 1593; and Henry Wilson had a John Shaxpere arrested for trespass in 1593. Adrian Quiney and others brought suits against a John Shaxspere for debt in 1591 and 1595, but both were against the shoemaker on his bonds to repay loans from Thomas Oken's bequest. John Shackspere of Stratford, corviser, sold his Balsall copyhold in 1596 and was not heard of again in Stratford.[15]

Shakespeare's father became surety for his brother Henry on June 4, 1586, and when Nicholas Lane sued him as surety in 1586/7, he obtained bail from Alderman Richard Hill and then secured a writ of habeas corpus to remove the case to Queen's Bench. His attorney in this suit, William Court (1549–1634), also wrote a deed for him in 1597 and was his attorney in the Common Pleas in 1599. At Coventry on July 19, 1586, John Shakespere of Stratford, glover, gave bail for Michael Pryce, of Stratford, tinker, to answer an indictment for felony before the justices of Queen's Bench; when Pryce did not appear, John forfeited ten pounds. Master John Shakespeare priced the goods of his neighbor Ralph Shaw, "Woll dryver," in July, 1592, and of Henry Field, tanner, in August, 1592. He signed Field's inventory with a cross and was called "m^r John Shaksper" and "John

Shaksper senior" to distinguish him from the shoemaker. "Master"
in the Stratford records meant one who had served as alderman or
who was otherwise entitled to be called gentleman.[16]

"M[r] John Shackspeare" was named in two lists of recusants in
Warwickshire in 1592, one made about March, the other dated
September 25 and signed by Sir Thomas Lucy and other justices.
The Privy Council had appointed commissioners to report "all
such as refused obstinately to resort to the church." The presenters
at Stratford, probably the churchwardens, listed Catholics who did
not come to church and then wrote: "Wee suspect theese nyne
personns next ensuinge absent themselues for feare of processes.
M[r] John Wheeler. John his ssonne. m[r] John Shackspeare. m[r]
Nycholas Barnehurste. Tho: James alias Giles. William Baynton.
Rychard Harington. William Fluellen. George Bardell." The
commissioners reported in September that certain Catholics had
conformed or promised to conform but only repeated what the
presenters had said about these nine: "It is sayd that these laste
nine coom not to Churche for feare of processe for Debtte." None
of the nine is known to have been either a Catholic or a Puritan
recusant, and none appears on the recusant roll of 1593. Barnhurst was an alderman and Wheeler and Shakespeare were former
aldermen. Fear of process was a common reason for not coming to
church, since sheriff's officers often made arrests on Sunday, when
most people could be found at church. The presenters at Tachbrook
in 1592 explained that Thomas Olney the elder "cometh not to the
church for feare of Processes, but he receveth the communion
yearely." Even a clergyman might not come to church, like the
rector of Week St. Mary in Cornwall in 1586 who "keepeth his
house for debt." Shakespeare's father had good reason to fear
arrest, for he had never paid the debt of seven pounds and damages which William Burbage had recovered against him in 1589.
When he failed to appear before the justices of the Common
Pleas in April, 1592, they ordered the sheriff of Warwickshire to
execute the judgment against him. Most of the others named with

him were also in debt. The elder Wheeler had his goods distrained to pay two creditors in 1590 and to pay John Lane, jr., in March, 1591/2, before he died in November, 1592. The younger Wheeler, sued for debt in 1590 by Thomas Trussell and by Ananias Nason, and in 1593 by John Lane, jr., was not prospering in 1599, when his house was "very ruinous" and his barn "readi to fall for rottennes." Sir Edward Greville sued him in 1601. A judgment was awarded against Barnhurst in 1591, and his goods were distrained to pay George Badger in March, 1591/2. Thomas Jones alias Giles ("James" is an error) was sued in 1591, 1592, and 1593 and died in the almshouse in 1614, while Harrington was sued in 1593 and each of the next five years and Baynton in 1594 and 1595. Baynton and Fluellen died in 1595. Writs of arrest were issued against Bardell in 1588 and 1592, and he described his debts in a Chancery suit of 1591 against Adrian and Richard Quiney, his brother-in-law William Baynton, William Court, Abraham Sturley, and Henry Walker. He had been partner with Charles Baynton as a mercer "in country term," William Court deposed (meaning one who was both mercer and grocer). Unable to pay a bond of six hundred pounds to Stephen Soame, alderman of London, Baynton "began to keep his house," was arrested but made a rescue, and fled to Ireland, where he was said to have died. Soame sued in the Common Pleas and had Bardell arrested for the debt. The undersheriff of Warwickshire, Basil Trymnell, at first let Bardell drink in a tavern at Warwick but when warned that he might escape kept him "in a more Strayter manner" and secured him by "a Locke with a Longe yron Chayne and a greate clogge." When Bardell was free again, it was no wonder he kept away from church for fear of arrest. Sent to prison again in December, 1592, he procured a certiorari. Both Bardell and Fluellen died poor, since Fluellen's widow was admitted to the almshouse in 1604, and Bardell's widow lived "in the Roomes over the Almesfolkes." John Shakespeare, then, was not attending church in 1592 for the reason given by his fellow townsmen: because he feared arrest for debt.[17]

Shakespeare's mother was called as a witness in 1596 in a suit by Robert Reade against John Sadler in the court of record. These names appear on the back of the jury list: "Maria Shaxpere Jur, Jone Reade, Jane Baker—Jur" (*iurata*, sworn). Reade, a surgeon, claimed that Sadler had promised but not paid him ten pounds for curing Sadler's friend John Gibbs, who had been wounded by a fall of timber on his head on June 10, 1595. Since Sadler denied the promise, the case went to a jury in July, 1596. Sadler was partner and neighbor to Gibbs, who in 1582 had a house in Rother Street with twenty-two elms and an orchard in Henley Lane with twenty-six elms and twelve ash trees.[18]

Shakespeare's father was probably the "m^r Shaxpere" mentioned in another document from the court of record. Robert Young's widow Margaret, whose daughters received legacies in 1624 by the will of her brother Richard Field the printer, sued for the value of goods which on July 20, 1595, she declared, came to the hands of Joan Perrott, widow, who on August 25 disposed of them to her own use. According to a note made in 1596, these goods included "m^r Shaxpere one boke. m^r barber a Coverlett ij daggars the 3 bokes. Ursula Fylld the apparell, & the bedding Clothes at whytsontyd was twelmonth." The original complaint specified three prayer-books worth ten shillings but did not give the name or value of the book apparently bought by "m^r Shaxpere." A jury found that the plaintiff had been "damnyfyd" in the sum of £5 9s. 4d. Joan Perrott, a poor relation of the late Alderman Perrott, was admitted to the almshouse in 1609. Thomas Barber of the Bear Inn was bailiff in 1594–95. Margaret Young's mother, Ursula, was the widow of Henry Field, whose goods had been appraised by John Shakespeare.[19]

On January 26, 1596/7, John Shakespeare, yeoman, sold for fifty shillings to George Badger, draper, a "toft" on the west side of his property in Henley Street. Since the toft was a strip of land described in the deed as only half a yard wide and twenty-eight yards long from Henley Street to the highway on the north called "Gyllpyttes," Badger may have wanted to build a wall. From this deed it has been assumed that John Shakespeare owned a third house, which was burnt in 1594; but this house is merely imaginary. He owned two houses in 1590, and there is no evidence that either was damaged by fire. He also sold a piece of land on the east, seventeen feet each way, to Edward Willis of King's Norton, Worcestershire, who was converting two small houses into an inn called the Bell. The date of this sale was "about fortie yeares" before a lawsuit of 1638.[20]

John and Mary Shakespeare were engaged in their Chancery suit against John Lambert from 1597 to 1599, and John in his own name brought another suit against Lambert. In the summer of 1599 he sued John Walford of Marlborough, Wilts, in the Common Pleas to recover a debt of twenty-one pounds, with damages of ten pounds. He said that the twenty-one pounds were payable on demand for twenty-one tods of wool (a tod weighed twenty-eight pounds) which he had sold to Walford at Stratford on November 4, 1568. Walford, who denied the debt, was a clothier and three times mayor of Marlborough.[21]

In 1601 a note by Richard Quiney of men who could testify to the rights of the borough which were being challenged by the lord of the manor, Sir Edward Greville, named "m^r Jhon Jefferryes, m^r Adrian Quyney, m^r Thomas Barber alias dier, m^r Jhon Sackesper, Symon Biddle, George Clemson, Jhon hemming." Jeffreys was steward of Stratford, Clemson was the bellringer, Heming was the beadle, and the others were old inhabitants.[22]

"Mr Johannes Shakspeare" was buried at Stratford on September 8, 1601, and his widow Mary on September 9, 1608. Thomas Plume wrote about 1657, when he set down some anecdotes of Shakespeare: "He was a glovers son—Sir John Mennis saw once his old Father in his shop—a merry Cheekd old man—that said— Will was a good Honest Fellow, but he durst have crackt a jeast with him at any time." Mennis was not born until 1599, but he may have been quoting someone else who had seen John Shakespeare.[23]

If Shakespeare's father left a last will and testament, it should have been proved in the peculiar court of the vicar, provided all his property was in the parish of Stratford. More likely he left no will and either his widow or one of his five children administered his estate. Wills and inventories from the vicar's court are at the Birthplace Library, with several bonds by administrators, but only a few grants of administration remain. Mary Shakespeare and some of her children probably continued to live in the western house, but by 1616 only William and Joan survived and William owned both of his father's houses in Henley Street.[24]

CHAPTER III

NEIGHBORS

IN STRATFORD

❖Shakespeare's first journey from home was to Stratford church, where "Gulielmus filius Johannes Shakspere" was christened on April 26, 1564. The day of his birth is not known, but children were usually baptized within a few days of birth. The vicar who probably christened him, John Bretchgirdle of Christ Church, Oxford, M.A., died in 1565. His will bequeathed many books: to the scholars of Stratford school *Bibliotheca Eliotae,* the Latin-English dictionary of Sir Thomas Elyot revised by Thomas Cooper; to a godson, Horace and Virgil; and to five sons of Alderman William Smith, Aesop, Cicero's *Offices* in English, Sallust, Justin, *Apophthegmata,* the *Copia Verborum* of Erasmus, David's *Psalms,* and three copies of *The Acts of the Apostles,* translated into English meter by Christopher Tye, Doctor in Music, with notes "to synge and also to play upon the Lute."[1]

Shakespeare was probably born in Henley Street, either in the western house now called the Birthplace or in the eastern house next to it. John Shakespeare had a house in Henley Street in 1552, either as owner or tenant. In 1556 he bought the eastern house and another house in Greenhill Street; in 1575 he bought two houses somewhere in Stratford; and in 1590 he held both the eastern house and the larger western house. He may have bought the

western house before Shakespeare was born, or it may have been
one of the houses which he bought in 1575.[2]

Though the early years of Shakespeare are unrecorded, something can be learned about the people who were living in Stratford
at this time. He probably knew most of them from about 1570 to
1585, and nearly all have left traces in the borough records, in
the parish registers, or in wills and other manuscripts. Many of the
townsmen, with the streets where they lived, are named in a rent
roll of town property in 1574 or in the survey of those who held
Stratford freeholds from the Earl of Warwick before 1590. Fitting
one piece of evidence to another will introduce us to certain
dwellers in the town when Shakespeare was a boy.

As Shakespeare grew up, he would have known his neighbors
in Henley Street. Next door on the east lived William Wedgewood, tailor, who in 1575 sold to Edward Willis of King's
Norton two houses between those of John Shakespeare and
Richard Hornby. A deed in 1573 by which Wedgewood sold land
to Hornby was witnessed by John Shakespeare, Roger Green, and
John Ainge, and Shakespeare's father also witnessed the deed of
1575. Wedgewood sold to John Tomlins, tailor, in 1574 his shop-
board, yard measure, and pressing iron, and he was still suing
Tomlins in 1586. He had been banished from Warwick by the
Earl of Warwick, who "pluckid his livery from him," and "leaving his wief he went to Stretford & divers other places & there
marryed an other wief his first wief yet living besides that he is a
man very contencious prowde & slaunderous oft busieng himself
with noughty matters & quarelling with his honest neighbours
which condicions forcing him to leave place of good government
first went from hence & afterward was compellid to goo from
Stretford." Next in Henley Street were the house and smithy of
Richard Hornby, who was made free of the Smiths' company in
1568–69 and was constable in 1584. He made links and staples
"for the seriauntes to make fast their prisoners." His early sixteenth-century house is now an office for the Birthplace Trust.
Hornby married in 1564 and had children, Joan, Thomas, Roger,

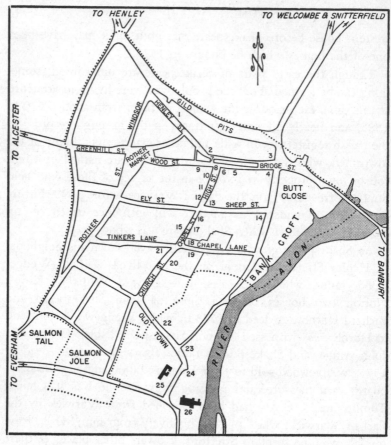

Stratford upon Avon

........Boundaries of the borough

1	Birthplace	14	William Tyler
2	Angel	15	William Court
3	Swan	16	Thomas Reynolds
4	Bear	17	July Shaw
5	Crown	18	New Place
6	Cage	19	Chapel
7	Middle Row	20	Gild Hall and School
8	High Cross	21	John Sadler
9	Hill, Sturley	22	Hall's Croft
10	Adrian Quiney	23	William Reynolds
11	William Smith, mercer	24	Thomas Greene
12	Thomas Rogers	25	College
13	Hamnet Sadler	26	Church

Anne, and Francis. Gilbert Bradley, glover, tenant of the next house in 1561, was chosen a burgess in 1565 and may have been godfather in that year to Gilbert, son of Humphrey Reynolds, and in 1566 to Gilbert Shakespeare. In 1562 he sued John Crochyn for payment for a gelding and saddle and John Medes for borrowing cap knives, sword hilts, and dagger hilts. Bradley's house was occupied in 1574 by William Wilson, whittawer, later bailiff, who rebuilt it after it was burnt in 1594. By this house a stream called the Mere ran across Henley Street and down Mere Pool Lane to the Rother Market. A miller in Henley Street, Roger Green, was fined for taking too much toll, for selling candles lacking weight, and for making "unwholsum aell." He had a garden in "hell lane" (also called Henley Lane or Windsor Lane). Henley Street was full of children, for John Ainge, baker, had seven children, including twins, and George Ainge, mercer, had fourteen children, including two sets of twins. George Ainge the younger, born in 1569, became a citizen and skinner in London.[3]

The bailiff when Shakespeare was born, George Whateley, owned a house and a woolendraper's shop in Henley Street with glass windows in the hall, parlor, and upper chamber, beehives in the garden, and "wax honey and other things in the apple chamber." Although he himself could not write, in 1586 he endowed a school at his native town, Henley in Arden, to teach thirty children reading, writing, and arithmetic. At the east end of the street, next the High Cross, lived William Smith, haberdasher and mercer, one of the chamberlains for whom John Shakespeare acted from 1563 to 1565. When John was removed from office in 1586, Smith refused to serve as alderman or to attend meetings, so that the council removed him also. Though he was reported in 1589 to have had no goods to seize for debt, when he died in 1600 his goods were valued at £169 10s., including corn in his fields at Bishopton, eight oxen, and a dozen cattle. Shakespeare would have known his five sons, three of whom were chosen bailiff, John Smith, vintner, Francis, and Henry.[4]

The house just west of the Shakespeares, probably let to tenants, was owned by Thomas Badger and then by his son George, a

draper who lived in Sheep Street. John Shakespeare rode to Warwick in 1572 as a juror to inquire into the estate left by Thomas
Badger, miller, of Bidford Grange, and ten years later he and
William Burbage chose William Badger as an arbiter. John
Wheeler took a lease of two houses in Henley Street in 1560 and
owned two others in 1590. He was bailiff in 1565 and 1576 and
chief alderman when John Shakespeare and Nicholas Barnhurst
were bailiffs, resigned his office as alderman in 1586, and was
presented in 1592, with his son John and John Shakespeare, for
not coming to church. Peter Smart of Henley Street became a
burgess in 1571 and an alderman in the last year of his life, 1588.
Shakespeare's father appraised the goods in 1592 of Ralph Shaw,
dealer in wool, who named to oversee his will his "loving neighbours" in Henley Street, Valentine Tant (married in 1577, d.
1616) and William Smart, a son of Peter. Shaw, who had married
in 1570, left two sons, Shakespeare's friend July and William, a
glover who succeeded to the Henley Street house when his mother
married the schoolmaster, Mr. Aspinall.[5]

As Shakespeare walked down the north side of Bridge Street
from Henley Street towards the Avon, he would come first to the
Angel, leased in 1555 by Alderman Ralph Cawdrey alias Cooke.
Cawdrey had butcher shops opposite, behind the Shambles in
Middle Row, where shops divided the broad street. He was bailiff
in 1556, 1567, and 1581, but he was also presented for frays and
John Shakespeare had him bound to keep the peace in 1582, when
he must have been over sixty. By that year he had leased the
Angel to Arthur Newall, and his will in 1588 left another house
in Bridge Street where Mr. Thomas Trussell, attorney, dwelt.
Trussell and John Shakespeare four years later appraised the goods
of Richard Field's father Henry, a tanner in Bridge Street. Trussell's own goods were valued at only forty-four shillings, and his
widow Magdalen was imprisoned for debt. Richard Ange, baker
in Bridge Street, wore sword and dagger at Warwick musters in
1577, became a burgess in 1590, and sued Henry Shakespeare the
next year. The Swan Inn near the bridge was kept by Thomas

Dixon alias Waterman, whose mother was Joan Townsend from Snitterfield. Dixon married in 1559 Philip, widow of John Burbage, vintner. He was sued in Chancery in 1571 for refusing the office of alderman and paid a fine in 1585 rather than act as bailiff, but served as alderman from 1584 to 1590. At the Swan the corporation entertained Bishop Whitgift, the Earl of Warwick, and Thomas Cartwright with wine and sugar. The inventory of Dixon's goods in 1603 mentions rooms in the inn, the Lion, the Talbot, and the Cock.[6]

On the south side of Bridge Street, called Fore Bridge Street, stood the Bear Inn, opposite the Swan. Alderman Thomas Barber alias Dyer of the Bear was three times bailiff and lived until 1615. He provided claret and sack in 1581 and 1583 for Sir Fulke Greville and other guests of the town. The house next the Bear was bought in 1567 by Richard Godwin, smith. He used "obprobryous woordes" to the bailiff in 1556 but later was paid for mending the jail and the chapel bell. The Crown Inn was occupied in 1574 by Richard Sponer, painter, who helped John Shakespeare to appraise the goods of Henry Field. Anthony Tanner, a tanner in Bridge Street, left Stratford in 1578 without paying the town all that he had collected as chamberlain.[7]

Middle Row, or the Shop Row, divided Fore Bridge Street from Back Bridge Street and the beginning of Wood Street from Henley Street. Among others it contained in 1574 three shops of William Smith, haberdasher, three of Ralph Cawdrey, and two of George Pynder, goldsmith. In 1585 Smith leased another shop, "the house at the crosse." Christopher Smith alias Court kept a tavern in Middle Row between Bridge Street and High Street and lent money to Henry Shakespeare. William Greenway, the carrier of goods to and from London, also kept a draper's shop, with his wife Ursula, daughter of Ralph Cawdrey. Ralph Bott or Boote, buttonmaker, had the last shop in the row, facing Henley Street.[8]

In Wood Street, the next street to Henley Street, lived Richard Hill, woolendraper, chosen bailiff in the plague year of 1564 and two later years. A friend in need to John Shakespeare, who had served with him as arbiter in 1559, he gave bail when John was arrested in 1587. His son-in-law Abraham Sturley and the vicar witnessed his will, and he was praised on his monument in English and Latin verse, with further inscriptions in Greek and Hebrew. Basil Burdett, bricklayer, had a house nearby and Humphrey Cowper, corviser, lived next to the house and garden of John Edwardes, laborer. The house with a gable still standing at the corner of Wood Street and Rother Street was occupied by John Page, ironmonger, until his death in 1580 and then by William Parsons, draper, bailiff in 1590 and 1611, and father of a son at Balliol. Parsons sold "Sea grene kersye" and broadcloth of orange tawny, green, violet in grain, peach, and "muske culler."[9]

Robert Perrott, a rich brewer, leased the tavern called King's Hall or King's House in Rother Market, now the White Swan, with sixteenth-century wall-paintings of Tobias and Raphael which were rediscovered in 1927. His son-in-law Thomas Brogden, draper and burgess, was host of the tavern in 1578. Perrott was bailiff in 1558 but refused to serve in 1567 and made a vow never to be of the corporation, though Sir Thomas Lucy, Clement Throckmorton, and Henry Goodere ordered that all parties "from henceforthe be Lovers and ffrendes." His characteristically Puritan will left Luscombe manor in Snitterfield to his grandson Ezechias Woodward, who had studied at Oxford, and gave money for the poor, for the preacher of a yearly sermon, and for the corporation "to make merye withall after the sermon is ended." His example in endowing a yearly sermon was later followed by Hamlet Smith and by Shakespeare's friends John and Thomas Combe.[10]

John Gibbs of Rother Street, who married in 1568 and was four times bailiff, was another Puritan, for he wrote "christyde" instead of "Christmas" in his accounts as chamberlain in 1590. He was hurt by a fall of timber in 1595, when Mary Shakespeare was called as a witness, but he lived for another thirty years and left an estate worth three hundred pounds, inventoried by John Wolmer, Richard Hathaway, and Richard Tyler. Among his neighbors in Rother Street were Ralph Downes, who had two houses and twenty-six elms, Matthew Bromley, whom John Shakespeare sued in 1559, and Thomas Hunt, who kept an alehouse. William Hill was ordered to make a chimney in his house to save the town from danger of fire.[11]

In Greenhill Street were the house and orchard of John Henshaw, who was fined for drawing his dagger in 1557. "Goodman Hinshowe" gilded the hand and dial (with a Tudor rose) of the town clock, and the bell was tolled in 1585 for "olde Hynchowe." John Shakespeare owned a house in Greenhill Street, but his tenants are not recorded. The borough tenants in this street were poor men, such as Hugh Pigeon, admitted an almsman in 1573, and Edmund Berry, who entered "the charytye house" in 1585.[12]

William Batha or Bathaway, laborer, lived in Ely Street and Thomas Attforde, shoemaker, later an almsman, had a house there with twelve elms. Philip Green, chandler and town chamberlain, leased a house there in 1580. He married Ursula, daughter of John Burbage, bailiff, and was a friend of John Shakespeare the corviser, who named children Ursula and Philip.[13]

In High Street, on the west side near Wood Street, lived one of the chief men of Stratford, Adrian Quiney, mercer. His father Richard and his grandfather Adrian had been masters of the Stratford gild and his grandson Thomas was later to marry Judith Shakespeare. The name was often pronounced "Queeny," as it was spelled in the baptismal and marriage records of Thomas. Richard and John "Qwenay" and their wives joined the gild of Knowle in 1480. Adrian had a son Richard and two daughters when in 1557 he married a second wife, the widow of Laurence Baynton, and moved from Henley Street to her house in High Street. He rebuilt this house after a fire in 1582 and again after the fires of 1594 and 1595. One of the original aldermen in the charter of 1553, he was bailiff in 1559, 1571, and 1582, and lived until 1607. A house which he rented next door was occupied in 1574 by his stepson Charles Baynton, whose wares ranged from sugarloaves to gunpowder. On the other side of Quiney's house John Smith, vintner, kept a tavern, where he furnished wine and cakes for Sir Fulke

Greville and for the Earl of Warwick. He married Hamnet Sadler's sister Margaret in 1572 and was bailiff in 1598, when Sturley wrote that he "doth baily it exceeding many of his predecessors, beyond all expectation well." Apples and pears grew in his orchard at the end of Church Street.[14]

The New House in High Street was the home of Alderman William Smith, mercer and linendraper, who had been master of the gild in 1540. By his second wife, Alice, sister of John Watson, later Bishop of Winchester, he had six sons, all named in the will of John Bretchgirdle, vicar. After he retired and went to live at Worcester in 1577, the house was occupied by his son John, ironmonger, bailiff in 1604. Alice Smith's will bequeathed the glass and wainscot in the New House, and the wainscot still covers the walls. Simon Biddle succeeded his father Henry, an alderman, as a cutler in High Street and was paid for dressing the town pikes and bows. He was named with John Shakespeare in 1601 as a witness to the rights of the town.[15]

Thomas Rogers, butcher, a great buyer of cattle and of barley for malt, had three wives and many children, of whom Katherine became the mother of John Harvard. He was ale-taster in 1569 and bailiff in 1589 and in 1595, when he entertained Sir Thomas Lucy. After the fire of 1594 he rebuilt his house in High Street, now the Harvard House, with the finest carved wood in the town, including grotesque faces, a bull's head, and a bear and ragged staff. The house next door, also rebuilt after the fire and now the Garrick Inn, was rented by Thomas Deege alias Gethen, weaver, whose mark was a sword (*degen* in Dutch and German). His wife Joan died of plague in 1564 and "Father Deege" died in the almshouse in 1597.[16]

On the east side of High Street, at the corner of Sheep Street, lived Roger Sadler, baker, bailiff in 1560 and 1572. When he died in 1578 he left his estate to his wife Margaret and his kinsman Hamnet Sadler. Among his debtors were Richard Hathaway of Shottery and sureties for John Shakespeare. Another debtor was Lewis ap Williams of High Street, ironmonger and innholder, bailiff in 1561 and 1573. He married Joan, daughter of John Burbage, and had a son Lewis of Shakespeare's age. Borough tenants on the east side of the street in 1574 included William Trout for two tenements and a chamber over the jail, and Anthony Wolston, butcher, for the Cage. The Cage, a former prison at the corner of Bridge Street, was now a house.[17]

In Sheep Street, on the north side near High Street, lived Humphrey Plumley, mercer, bailiff in 1562 and 1574. When he sealed a deed and bond for Thomas Oken's bequest in 1575, John Fisher, the town clerk of Warwick, described Plumley and his comrades from Stratford as "men known of good credit, honest behaviour, upright dealing," and so the money was paid "and they of Stratford sent merry homewards." He signed as "Plomley" a lease naming his neighbor Robert Hynd, whom he had sued in 1553. Hynd, called chapman in 1562 and haberdasher in his will in 1588, brought goods by packhorse from Birmingham and leased a shop at Shipston on Stour, which he left to his son Humphrey. Twice he sued men who accused him of stealing, once a pack of sieves and another time timber, "more lyker a theyfe then a trew man."[18]

George Badger, woolendraper, also lived in Sheep Street, though he owned a house in Henley Street next to John Shakespeare's. He married Alice Court in 1578 and had sixteen children, of whom he apprenticed George to himself when the boy was nearly fourteen and bound Richard at sixteen to Peter Short, stationer of London. Chosen an alderman in 1594, he was removed in 1598 for refusing to attend or to serve as bailiff. Nicholas Barnhurst or Bannister, alderman in 1577 and bailiff in 1579, was also a woolendraper, but no friend to his next-door neighbor, Badger. For calling Badger "knave & rascall" in 1596 he was threatened with removal from the council, and he was expelled in 1599 "for his great abuse offered to the whole Company." He married in 1562 Elizabeth Baynton, stepdaughter to Adrian Quiney, and had eleven children, of whom six died young. In 1582 he arbitrated between John Shakespeare and William Burbage. Like John Shakespeare, he was presented in 1592 for not coming to church. His neighbor Richard Boyce was warden of the Tailors and Shearmen in 1569, and Richard Nichols was a whittawer. Mrs. Margaret Jeffreys, an alderman's widow, lived in the old Shrieve's House, which still stands as it was rebuilt after 1595 when Sheep Street was destroyed by fire. John Taylor, shearman, rented a house in Sheep Street and a barn in Bancroft Side. As chamberlain with John Shakespeare from 1561 to 1563 he made his mark, a pair of calipers. Across the way on the south side near the Bancroft lived William Tyler, butcher (1525–89), constable with John Shakespeare, chamberlain from 1563 to 1565, bailiff in 1577 and 1585, and father of Shakespeare's friend Richard Tyler.[19]

Mr. Thomas Reynolds, father of another friend of Shakespeare, had a large house in Chapel Street, now part of the Shakespeare Hotel, as well as a farm near the church. He and his wife Margaret, Catholic recusants in 1592, had thirteen children baptized at Stratford, and, with servants, a household of twenty-two persons in 1595. Mr. Walter Roche resigned the mastership of the school in 1571 but continued to live in Chapel Street, three doors from New Place. Robert Gibbs, who became a sergeant at mace in 1579, lived next door, in the house later July Shaw's. New Place was owned by Mr. William Underhill until he sold it to Shakespeare. A gatehouse and shop across the way were occupied by William Brace, draper, and then by William Court, attorney for John Shakespeare in 1587 and 1599.[20]

The gild chapel, the grammar school, and the almshouses in Church Street were all built or rebuilt in the fifteenth century. Robert Hall, freemason, leased the Old School in the chapel grounds, later the schoolmaster's house. Beyond the row of almshouses lived Robert Salisbury, brewer, bailiff in 1569 and two later years, who had four houses and thirty-six elms. Next door was the vicar's house, occupied from 1569 to 1584 by Mr. Henry Heicroft. John Sadler, miller, had a large freehold in Church Street near Scholars' Lane, with stables, dovehouses, orchards, and gardens, and also leased the town mills on the Avon below the church. Bailiff in 1570, he declined the office in 1582, when John Shakespeare voted for him, and died in 1582/3.[21]

The one stone house in Stratford, the College, was the residence of John Combe, as it had once been of the warden and four other priests who made up a college of clergy. This John Combe, who died in 1588, was bailiff of the two Stratford manors for the Earl of Warwick and secured a grant of arms in 1584. He had at least seven children by his first wife and seven by his second. The first Mrs. Combe was Joyce Blount of Worcestershire, aunt of Sir Christopher Blount and cousin of another Joyce Blount who married Hugh Reynolds and became the mother of Thomas Reynolds. For his second wife Combe married in 1561 Rose, daughter of William Clopton. Her brother William owned Clopton House and the Dower House in Old Town, a street near the College. The younger William Clopton and his wife Anne were recusants, and their monument in the church shows them with seven children, of whom the only ones living when their father died in 1592 were Joyce, wife of Sir George Carew, and Anne, wife of William Clopton of Durham. Clopton House, north of Stratford, had a park, with a keeper who was buried in 1580.[22]

William Clopton is the only esquire at Stratford in "A Booke of the Names and Dwelling Places of the Gentlemen and Freeholders in the Countye of Warwicke 1580." The sheriff's jurymen were probably to be chosen from this list. Three Stratford men are described as gentlemen, Nicholas Bannister (because he was then bailiff), John Combe, and William Underhill. The list names John Shakespeare and all his brother aldermen except William Tyler and Robert Salisbury; among the chief burgesses Thomas Dixon, John Smith, William Brace, Philip Green, and Peter Smart; and other freeholders including Nicholas and John Lane and George and William Badger. Richard Woodward was listed under Shottery. A similar list of 1572 names John Shakespeare, Thomas Shakespeare of Stratford (marked "quene"), and Thomas Shakespeare of Warwick. Henry Ferrers of Baddesley Clinton drew up another survey of Warwickshire lords, knights, esquires, and gentlemen in 1577–78. He named four gentlemen at Stratford: "Thomas Coombes" (evidently John Combe), Nicholas and John Lane, and William Underhill. Clopton, Underhill, and Nicholas Lane were among the gentlemen ordered to send horsemen to Tilbury in 1588.[23]

Nicholas Lane filled his coffers by purchasing land, amassing such wealth that when he died in 1595 he could afford a portrait tomb in Alveston church. His son Richard bought Alveston manor in 1603 from Sir Edward Greville and became Richard Lane, esquire, with a son at Oxford. Both men were well known to the Shakespeares. Nicholas lent money to Henry Shakespeare and sued John. Richard witnessed a deed for John Shakespeare in 1597, was chosen one of his commissioners the next year, and joined William Shakespeare in bringing a Chancery suit. Richard was born about 1556, when he was named in a will, and I find him testifying in 1586, aged thirty, that he had been a suitor to marry Justice Windham's sister Jane, widow of John Pope of Wroxton, Oxfordshire, but that she said he was too young a man for her. He married Joan Whitney of Mitcham, Surrey, a recusant in 1592, as was his uncle John Lane the elder (d. 1600). The Lanes were men of hot temper. Old Nicholas attacked an enemy at Henley in Arden in 1592 with a crabtree cudgel. His nephew Nicholas quarreled in 1601 with Francis Bellars of the Bear and in 1604 was killed with a cowlstaff by Robert Fisher, shoemaker, who was indicted for murder but acquitted because he struck *se defendendo*. Nicholas, aged thirty-five but unmarried, was buried as "Nicoles Lane, adolocentulus." Shakespeare's daughter Susanna sued for slander John Lane, a grandson of old Nicholas. It is fitting that the family arms in 1619 were three fireballs, flaming.[24]

Stratford had nine vicars during Shakespeare's lifetime. John Bretchgirdle, M.A. of Oxford, bequeathed many books when he died in 1565. William Smart, a former fellow of Christ's, Cambridge, was schoolmaster from 1554 to 1565 and vicar from 1565 to 1567. William Butcher, not to be confused with two men of the same name at Oxford, was replaced in 1569 by Henry Heicroft,

fellow of St. John's, Cambridge, M.A. in 1570. Marrying Emme
Careless in 1571, he had five children baptized and three of them
buried at Stratford. He seems to have delivered special Lenten sermons in 1583, when the town paid "for a pound of candels which
M^r. Haycroft had when he preached a morninges." Next year he
left for Rowington, a richer benefice, where he had the parish buy
a book by the reformer Musculus. The Earl of Warwick then presented Richard Barton from Coventry, described in a Puritan survey as "a precher, learned, zealous, & godlie, & fit for the min-
isterie. A happie age yf our Church were fraight [with] manie
such." The council members did their best to keep him by making
many gifts beyond his salary of twenty pounds a year. Long after he
resigned, he came back to preach special sermons in 1597 and
1601. John Rushton was presented in February, 1589, and in
November John Bramhall, M.A., who served until he died in 1596.
The town councilors petitioned Burghley and the queen to free
him from paying first fruits and subsidies because the stipend was
so small and his cure at least three thousand souls. They paid him
the special fee left by Thomas Oken for preaching a sermon on
election day, and Alderman Hill left ten shillings "to Mr Broome-
hill for a sermon at my buriall." He may have provided the Hebrew and Greek carved on Hill's monument. Richard Byfield, presented in 1596/7 by Edward Greville, was rewarded with fees for
sermons, a quart of sack, and a lease of the churchyard. In 1600,
as a convocation of the clergy had ordered, he had the old paper
register transcribed on parchment, bound in leather with brass
clasps and bosses bearing the Tudor rose. He signed the register
through 1602 and a certificate for his curate in 1604, but under
James I he was inhibited from preaching. Several aldermen rode to
Bishop Babington to obtain a license for Byfield to preach at
Easter in 1605, and he received his salary for eight months of that
year. The council offered to appoint him associate to the schoolmaster, Richard Woodward's widow Frances and others conveyed
property to him in 1605/6, and the town gave him wine in 1608
and in 1617. In 1622 he had a house at Isleworth, Middlesex,

where his son Nicholas was vicar, and the widow of Nicholas left
him her husband's black silk cloak. He died there in 1633, naming
in his will his loving wife Margaret, whom he had married at Stratford in 1597, his son Richard, born at Stratford in 1598, and his
son Nathaniel, born at Stratford in 1602, to whom he left "all my
study of books." John Rogers, vicar of St. Nicholas, Warwick, was
presented by Sir Edward Greville and was instituted at Stratford
in June, 1605.[25]

A familiar figure in Stratford for over fifty years was William
Gilbard alias Higgs, the curate, who died in 1612. John Shakespeare paid him four pounds as under schoolmaster for 1561–62
and later chamberlains paid him as acting master for short periods
in several years from 1564 to 1574, so that he may have been one
of Shakespeare's first teachers. In 1575 the register calls him "assistant" and in 1576 William Gilbard, "clarke and assistent," was
receiving the curate's salary of ten pounds a year. "Sir William
Gilbard, Clarke and Curate," wrote the will of Richard Hathaway
in 1581 and many other wills, and he earned another pound a year
as keeper of the town clocks. The town paid "Ser Hydges" in
1601 for his boat hire to the court to speak with Mr. Fulke Greville. In 1602 he asked the town to keep two shillings a quarter out
of his wages to buy a Bible worth eight shillings which he would
bestow upon the chapel. He married three times and had ten children at Stratford and two baptized at Wootton Wawen. It has
been suggested that Shakespeare thought of Gilbard in describing
Sir Nathaniel the curate, that marvelous good neighbor. When his
license from the bishop was to be renewed in 1604, Byfield the
minister and eight aldermen wrote that they had known Gilbard
for many years "to be of a very honest, quiet, sober and good behaviour towards all men, and diligent to do all such things as are
required at his hands in his place, by the which behaviour he hath
well deserved both our loving affections and also these our letters
of commendations." He seems to have taken pride in his Latin, for
during the years when he signed the register, from 1603 to 1611,
the entries of baptisms and burials are unusually full of Latin

terms such as "Molendenarius," "elemozena," and "adolocentulus." These can hardly be attributed to the parish clerk, since different men held that office. John Pinder, the "Clarke" in 1583, was buried in 1605/6 as "edituus" or sexton, while Richard Green was buried in 1617 as "parish Clarke."[26]

CHAPTER IV

STRATFORD SCHOOL

✤According to Rowe, Shakespeare's father bred him "for some time at a Free-School," and there is no reason to doubt that this was the free grammar school of Stratford. Since Professor Baldwin has given full information on the studies and methods of Elizabethan schools, this chapter will discuss only the schoolmasters of Stratford in Elizabeth's reign and some of the boys who may have been schoolfellows of Shakespeare between about 1570 and 1580.

By their charter of 1553 the burgesses of Stratford were to pay the schoolmaster twenty pounds a year and provide him a dwelling. The new master, William Smart, agreed in 1555 to pay the old master, William Dalam, ten marks a year for his wages and after Dalam's death to pay four pounds a year for an usher or for repairs to the school. Dalam died in 1558. The town paid four pounds of the twenty "to alen for techyng ye chylder" for the year 1562–63 and three pounds for 1563–64, probably for three quarters of the year. William Gilbard alias Higgs was paid four pounds for 1561–62, 10s. 8d. for eight weeks' wages for 1563–64, and 10s. 8d. for the next year. From 1565 to the end of the century the schoolmasters received their full twenty pounds and the names of the ushers were not recorded. The townsmen petitioned Queen Elizabeth, however, for the right to "make the usher of their school." The council mentioned in 1622 that the master "mʳ Aspynall hath eleccion of An ussher out of his owne meanes," and this was probably the custom in Shakespeare's time. Abraham

The Schoolroom at Stratford

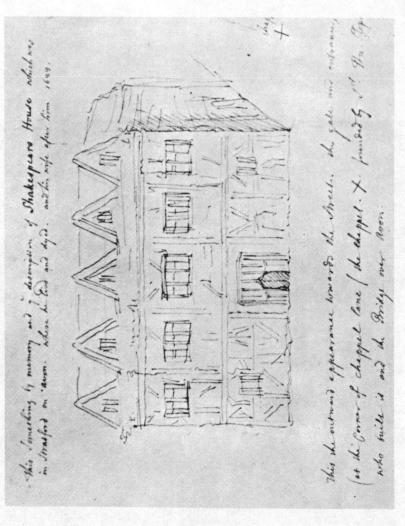

New Place

from a drawing by George Vertue

Sturley wrote in 1597 that his son Henry was about to begin teaching under Aspinall; Henry was then twenty and had entered Oxford in 1594/5. He took over from Gilbard a room in the school, and in 1600 the chamberlain "Paid the scolemaisters their wages." Aspinall chose other under schoolmasters, including Richard Quiney's son George, who was born in 1600, took his M.A. at Oxford in 1620, and became both usher and "reading minister" in 1622. Shakespeare may have studied under such young men from a university, but their names are not known.[1]

John Brownsword, who had taught at Macclesfield and Warwick, was master at Stratford from 1565 to 1567, after which he returned to Macclesfield in his native Cheshire. His Latin poems were published in 1590 by his pupil Thomas Newton, a translator of Seneca, and John Brinsley called him "that ancient Schoolemaster . . . so much commended for his order and Schollers."[2]

The next master, Mr. Acton, was succeeded by Walter Roche, master from Christmas, 1569, to Michaelmas, 1571. A Lancashire man, Roche was a fellow of Corpus Christi College, Oxford, in 1559, rector at Droitwich in 1569, and from 1574 to 1578 rector of Clifford Chambers, where his daughter Mary was christened in 1575. His house, in 1574 and 1582, was in Chapel Street near New Place. He witnessed deeds with John Shakespeare in 1573 and 1575 and gave surety in a marriage bond for William Parsons in 1578. Shakespeare may have entered school while he was master, but the younger boys would have been taught by the usher in the same room.[3]

Shakespeare was still a young scholar in the time of Simon Hunt, B.A. at Oxford in 1568, who was master from 1571 to 1575. The Bishop of Worcester licensed Hunt on October 29, 1571, to teach literature and instruct boys in Stratford grammar school. He paid his share in 1573 towards repairing the school windows, and he paid rent for his chamber from Michaelmas, 1574, to Michaelmas, 1575. One Simon Hunt matriculated at the University of Douai about July, 1575, became a Jesuit in 1578, served as English penitentiary or confessor at St. Peter's in succession to Robert Parsons, and died at Rome in 1585. The schoolmaster may have been the Jesuit, or he may have been the Simon Hunt of Stratford who died in or before 1598, when his estate of one hundred pounds was administered by Thomas Harward of Tardebigg, who had been overseer in 1578 of the will of Alderman Smith of Stratford and Worcester.[4]

Shakespeare's chief master at Stratford school was Thomas Jenkins, who taught there from 1575 to 1579. He was not born in Wales, as has been assumed, though other students named Jenkins came to Oxford from Wales and Monmouthshire as well as from English families in Somerset, Gloucestershire, and Sussex. A Londoner, son of an "old servant" of Sir Thomas White, founder of St. John's, Oxford, he took his B.A. in 1566 and his M.A. in 1570 and was fellow of St. John's from 1566 to 1572, when the college granted him a lease of "Chawser's Howse" at Woodstock. Sir Thomas White wrote to the college in December, 1566, requesting that Jenkins have leave of absence for two years "that he may give himself to teach children." In 1575 Stratford paid expenses "for a schole master that came from warwicke," and Jenkins paid rent for his chamber for part of this year. Later he rented two chambers, probably needing more room because he was married. "Jone daughter to Mr. Thomas Jenkes" was buried in 1576, and Thomas, son to Mr. Thomas Jenkins, was christened in 1578. The town paid "Mr Jenkins for implements & cariage" when the trained soldiers went to Warwick on June 8, 1579. He signed his name "Thomas Jenkens" on July 9, when he acknowledged receiving six pounds which his successor had agreed to give him "in consideracion of my departure from the schole of Stretford uppon Avon." Since the town authorities approved this agreement, Jenkins evidently left with their consent, after finding to succeed him a friend who had taken his degree in the same year.[5]

John Cottom, as he signed his name, was licensed to teach at Stratford on September 28, 1579. A graduate of Oxford in 1566, from Brasenose, he was "late of London" in 1579. At Christmas he was paid for teaching six months in 1579, but the town re-

quired him to pay back four pounds a year, probably as salary for
the usher. He resigned, or was asked to resign, some time after
Michaelmas, 1581. His younger brother Thomas, a Jesuit who
came from Rheims with a letter to John Debdale of Shottery, was
arrested in 1580, arraigned with Edmund Campion in November,
1581, and executed in 1582. John Cottom eventually inherited his
father's lands in Lancashire and became a Catholic recusant.[6]

Alexander Aspinall came as schoolmaster in 1582 and remained
until his death in 1624. His name was still remembered when Sir
Francis Fane (1611–1680) set down this posy in his commonplace
book:

> "The gift is small
> The will is all:
> A shey ander Asbenall.

Shaxpaire upon a peaire of gloves that mas[t]er sent to his mistris."

A pleasant fancy, which Fripp states as a fact, suggests that the
schoolmaster bought the gloves from John Shakespeare to give to
his betrothed before his marriage in 1594; and Fripp is equally
sure that Aspinall was the prototype of Holofernes in *Love's
Labour's Lost*. Born in Lancashire, Aspinall was at Brasenose in
1572 and proceeded B.A. in 1575 and M.A. in 1578. At Stratford
he lived at first in "the Schoolemasters Chamber" next the schoolroom in the gild hall, described in 1612 as "the Chambers over our
Council Chamber wheare Mr. Aspinall dwelled." After leasing
in 1590 three houses in the Chapel grounds, he chose to live in the
Old School, built about 1428, sometimes called the Pedagogue's
House. Here there was room for the wife he married in 1594,
Anne, widow of Ralph Shaw, and she evidently carried on the
business of her first husband, who had left her "xxj todde of
woll" and "vj todd of yearne." She was sued in 1593 on the
statute for wool trading. It was reported of Aspinall in 1595 that
"besides his office he hath the trades of buying and selling of wool
and yarn and making of malt and hath 32 quarters of malt." Because of the dearth of grain he was forbidden to make more malt

for sale, and he had only eleven quarters in 1598, when his neighbor Shakespeare had ten. The council voted in 1595 "that there shalbe no schole kept in the Chapell from this time following." Aspinall was chosen burgess in 1596, alderman in 1602, and the next year chamberlain and headborough of Chapel Street ward. When he was elected bailiff in 1606 he paid a fine rather than serve, and he paid another in 1614 for permission to resign as alderman; but he remained a councilman "in regard of his sufficiency for his contynuall advise & great experience in the Borough affairs" and was ranked first among the burgesses "in regard he is an auncient master of Art & a man lerned." In 1613 he became deputy keeper of the court of record and a deputy town clerk, often keeping the council minutes. Though his under master Richard Wright, just out of Brasenose, criticized his teaching in 1608, Aspinall sent many Stratford boys on to Oxford, and Henry Sturley and George Quiney came back to teach under him. The administration of his goods was granted in 1624 to his uncle, Alexander Aspinall, yeoman, of Clitheroe, Lancashire, and the town bought "a chaine for the booke which Mr. Aspinall gave to the scoole."[7]

The masters at Stratford left no record of their scholars, but a few of the Stratford boys near Shakespeare's age can be traced in later years. Of the twenty-eight boys christened at Stratford in 1564, one attended a university. "W. fil. W. Smith" was christened on November 22, 1564, and was named the following year in the will of John Bretchgirdle, vicar, who left books to five sons of William Smith, mercer and alderman, and a shilling "to Wyllam smithe the yongest sonne" (the eldest son was another William). His uncle John Watson, Bishop of Winchester, on October 23, 1583, left ten pounds each to his sister Smith and to every one of her children and twenty marks each "to William Smith her son the elder that is with me" and "to William Smith her son now Scholar in the College" (Winchester College). The only boy of this name who was a scholar at Winchester in the reign of Elizabeth was entered as William Smyth of Stratford upon Avon, though the school records seem to be mistaken in giving his age as twelve when he was elected a scholar in 1580. When "William Smythe" matriculated at Oxford on October 11, 1583, from Exeter College, he was described as of Worcestershire, son of a plebeian, and aged eighteen, which fits the age of the William born in 1564. The entry should mean that he was born in Worcestershire, but his father had removed to Worcester and died there by 1579 and his mother was living there in 1583. His brother Richard entered Christ Church at Oxford in 1572 and became a clergyman. Dr. Hotson found a deposition by William Smithe of Loughton, Essex, schoolmaster, B.A., aged twenty-four or thereabouts, who testified on May 12, 1589, that he was born in "Stretford upon haven," had studied letters for two years in the University of Oxford, and had lived for nearly a year in Waltham Cross and nearly a year in Loughton. This testimony makes it clear that the William Smith who was born at Stratford in 1564 graduated from Oxford. His nephew William Smith, born at Stratford in 1598, served the Czar and wrote from Russia asking the heralds to send him the arms which he claimed a right to bear as the son and grandson of Stratford aldermen (John Smith, ironmonger, and William Smith, mercer).[8]

Richard Field, baptized on November 16, 1561, was the son of Henry Field, the tanner of Bridge Street whose goods John Shakespeare appraised in 1592. Richard probably attended Stratford school before he was apprenticed on September 29, 1579, to George Bishop, stationer of London, who agreed that he should serve the first six years of his seven with Thomas Vautrollier, the Huguenot printer in Blackfriars. Here he was the only prentice, though Vautrollier was allowed French or Dutch workmen. Mrs. Jacqueline Vautrollier carried on the printing house while her husband was in Edinburgh, and after he died in 1587 she married Field. He took as prentice in 1591/2 the youngest of his seven brothers, Jasper, born in 1577. Field was both printer and publisher of Puttenham's *Art of English Poesy* (1589), of Sir John Harington's translation of *Orlando Furioso* (1591), and of Thomas Campion's *Poemata* (1596). He printed and published

Shakespeare's *Venus and Adonis* (1593) but sold the copyright in
1594 to John Harrison, for whom he printed later editions and
The Rape of Lucrece (1594). For William Ponsonby he printed
Chapman's *Shadow of Night* (1594), Spenser's *Faerie Queene* and
Four Hymns (1596), and Sidney's works in folio (1598). Besides
publishing many books about France and Italy, he printed works
in French, Italian, Spanish, and Welsh, with passages in Greek
and Hebrew. He lived and printed in the Blackfriars through
1610, and from 1615 at the Splayed Eagle in Wood Street. Master of the Stationers' Company in 1619 and 1622, he died in 1624,
leaving property to a later wife, Jane, and to his sons Richard and
Samuel. Richard signed for his portion when he came of age in
1640, Samuel in 1644, and a posthumous son Henry in 1645/6.
Other Stratford boys were also apprenticed to London stationers:
Roger, son of John Lock, glover, in 1577; Allen, son of Thomas
Orrians, tailor, in 1582/3; and Richard, son of George Badger,
draper, in 1602.[9]

John Sadler, born like Field in 1561, was the elder son of the
alderman for whom Shakespeare's father cast his vote for bailiff
in 1582. John married in 1584 Isabel, daughter of Peter Smart of
Henley Street. In 1595 he secured a surgeon for his friend John
Gibbs, and Shakespeare's mother testified when the surgeon sued
Sadler. With Gibbs as his partner he leased mills for grain and
malt, and he sued John Burman in 1605 for a share in a lease of
Charlecote mills and fishing from Sir Thomas Lucy. He looked
after the sons of his brother Thomas, who in 1601 went off to the
wars in Ireland. Bailiff in 1599 and 1612, he made his will in
1625 as John Sadler, gentleman. His son John became partner
with Richard Quiney the younger as a grocer in London and owner
of plantations in Virginia.[10]

Arthur Cawdrey was born in 1562 and his brother George in
1565. Their father, Alderman Ralph Cawdrey alias Cooke, brought
George into the council chamber in 1578 and had it proved and
recorded that the boy "at his age of iiij yeres had his left yere dis-
figured with [a] horse." Since this entry is the only one of its kind

at Stratford, there must have been special reason for it. I suggest that George was leaving home and that his father wanted official proof of his identity when he returned, just as scars were recorded to identify foreign students at Padua. A few years later George was studying in France. In 1583, I find, he entered the English seminary at Rheims, where he was confirmed by the Bishop of Soissons and received minor orders from the Cardinal of Guise. Next year "Georgius Cawdrie, adolescens bonus et pius," left for England because he was suffering great pain in his eyes and many other bodily ills. But he was again at Rheims in 1587, when he left for Deventer with the confessor to Sir William Stanley's regiment, which had gone over to the King of Spain, and he returned to Rheims in 1588. His father's will in that year named six other sons, but not George. The presenters at Stratford in 1592 suspected George to be "a Seminarye Preeste or a Jhesuite, But where he now is they knowe not." They presented his mother Joan and his sister Alice as recusants and his mother for harboring seminaries.[11]

Arthur Cawdrey, woolendraper, succeeded his father at the Angel in Bridge Street and was elected to the town council in 1598. After his first wife was buried in 1607 as "Mary Cawdry, Recusant," he married again, served as bailiff in 1625, and lived until 1637. As a freeholder of Welcombe he opposed enclosure in September, 1614, but not in November, like Shakespeare protected his right by covenants, which the enclosers did not keep, and in December surveyed the arable lands for the town. Next year he signed an agreement not to exchange lands for enclosure and told William Combe "that he would never consent without the Towne & that he hadd a house & other things more profitable to him then his Land was: & that he hadd rather loose his Land then loose their good willes."[12]

John Lane, born in 1562, appears in effigy on the monument in Alveston church of his father Nicholas Lane, gentleman. He married in 1584 Frances, daughter of Thomas Nash, and the visitation of 1619 names their children, Nicholas, John, Margaret, wife of John Greene, and Mary, wife of Henry Bushell. Either he or his uncle John (d. 1600) was bailiff to Edward Greville in 1592 for Stratford manor, and he served reluctantly on the town council from 1600 to 1604. His signature may be seen on a lease of 1604 from Sir George and Lady Carew. He supported the town's battle against enclosure, declaring "that he would never agree while he lyved." His grandson John Lane, merchant (1609–38), made his will in 1638 at Cyprus while waiting to take passage home on the *Unicorn* from Aleppo.[13]

Three of these boys remained in Stratford, while the other three went off to Oxford or Rheims or a printer's shop in the Blackfriars. There is no proof that any of them were at school with Shakespeare; they are only a few of the many Stratford boys who could have been. Of the friends whom Shakespeare mentioned in his will, the one most likely to have been at school with him was Richard Tyler, a butcher's son born in 1566. Richard had a brother Adrian, of whom nothing is known except that he was christened in 1562/3. Only one tradition mentions a boyhood friend of Shakespeare. John Aubrey heard from "some of the neighbours" at Stratford that "There was at that time another Butcher's son in this Towne, that was held not at all inferior to him for a naturall witt, his acquaintance & coetanean, but dyed young." If there is anything in the story, this boy might have been Adrian Tyler, or he might have been another butcher's son, such as George Cawdrey. We shall never know.[14]

CHAPTER V

SHAKESPEARE

AND ANNE HATHAWAY

❖Hewlands Farm, called since 1795 Anne Hathaway's Cottage, is not a cottage but a well-built farmhouse in Shottery, about a mile west of Stratford church. Oak beams of the fifteenth century or earlier support the roof between the hall of two twelve-foot bays and the fifteen-foot east wing of two stories. Stone fireplaces were built in the sixteenth century and an upper floor was added to make chambers over the hall. Two more bays of two stories were put up on the west, probably by Anne's brother Bartholomew.[1]

Richard Hathaway of Shottery, husbandman, by his will of September 1, 1581, left ten marks to his daughter Agnes to be paid to her at the day of her marriage. The evidence is reasonably clear that she was the Anne who married Shakespeare, for the same person was often called both Anne and Agnes. Richard's will called one of Thomas Hathaway's daughters Agnes, but she was baptized in 1577 as Anne; Philip Henslowe's will called his wife Agnes, but she was Anne in the record of her funeral; and Bartholomew Hathaway's will called his daughter Anne, but she was baptized as Annys. The writer of Richard's will, William Gilbard, married in 1560 Agnes Lyncian, who was buried in 1579 as Anne Gilbart, and Shakespeare's friend Thomas Russell married Agnes Digges, usually known as Anne. Agnes was commonly pronounced Annes and was so written in the will of Robert Arden and in the inventory of the goods of "Annes Ardenne" in 1581.[2]

Anne Shakespeare, according to the inscription on the brass which marks her grave, was "of the Age of .67. yeares" when she died on August 6, 1623. She was therefore born about 1556, before the records of baptisms at Stratford begin in 1558.

The Bishop of Worcester's register notes the granting of a license on November 27, 1582, for a marriage "inter Willelmum Shaxpere et Annam whateley de Temple grafton." The clerk who wrote this note made errors in other entries, such as writing Robert "Darby" for Robert "Bradeley." That he should have written "Annam Hathwey" is made almost certain by a bond dated November 28 concerning a license for "william Shagspere" to marry "Anne hathwey of Stratford in the Dioces of Worcester maiden," with one asking of the banns. The parish of Stratford, then as now, included Shottery. The sureties in this bond, Fulk Sandells and John Rychardson, both described as husbandmen of Stratford, promised to pay forty pounds to the bishop's chancellor, Richard Cosin, and his registrar, Robert Warmstry, if the requirements for a lawful marriage were not satisfied. The bond states these requirements: that there should appear no impediment by reason of precontract, consanguinity, or affinity; that no suit should have been begun concerning such impediment; that William should not solemnize the marriage without the consent of Anne's friends; and that William should pay the costs if any legal action were brought against Bishop Whitgift and his officers for licensing the marriage. Richard Hathaway in 1581 had named his neighbor Fulk Sandells as an overseer of his will, and Rychardson had been a witness. When the bridegroom was a minor, as Shakespeare was, the custom at Worcester was for sureties to be friends or kinsmen of the bride, to look after her interests.[3]

Before granting a license the bishop's officials required a fee, a bond, and two other documents, of which no examples have been found at Worcester for the sixteenth century: an allegation on oath by the applicant stating the names, residences, and occupations of the man and woman and of their parents and the reasons for seeking a license; and a certificate attesting the consent of parents or guardians on both sides when this was necessary. Since Shakespeare was only eighteen and could not legally marry without his father's permission, the officials probably required proof that John Shakespeare had consented to the marriage. The consent of the groom's father is not mentioned in Worcester bonds before 1589; but in 1611 Alexander Batcheler, curate of Bishopton in the parish of Stratford, wrote to an official at Worcester in behalf of Thomas Walker of Stratford and Katherine Kirby of Warwick: "There is no danger in the graunting of your licence . . . Parents of both sides are fullye agreed." In 1624 Richard Holder, curate of Bishopton, and William Greene of Bishopton signed a marriage bond to Thomas Wilson, vicar of Stratford, which stated that Greene was to be married in the church or chapel of Bishopton between eight and twelve in the morning. The bond was to be void if there should appear no impediment to the marriage of William Greene and Richard Holder (whose name was written by mistake instead of that of the bride) "And if they be of lawfull age and have the Consent of parents or governors." The same carelessness about naming the bride is found in a Stratford bond of 1625 where hasty filling in of blank spaces left for names made the bond void if "John Francis and Edmund Canninge may lawfully solemnize matrimony together."[4]

Shakespeare and Anne Hathaway had reason to hasten their marriage, since their first child was christened on May 26, 1583. They could have married after the usual asking of banns on three Sundays or holidays if the first banns had been asked by November 18, but banns were forbidden from Advent Sunday, December 2 in 1582, to January 13. The Stratford registers before 1585 record only two marriages in December, one on the first and Abraham Sturley's on December 11, 1575. Shakespeare and Anne Hathaway, having secured a license, could have had their one reading of the banns on November 30, St. Andrew's day, and could then have married at any time following. The vicar of Stratford at this time, Henry Heicroft, had himself obtained a license on May 15, 1571, permitting him to marry Emme Careless with one publishing of the banns at the time of marriage, and they were married on June 18. Though it is not a matter of record, it is certainly possible that Shakespeare and Anne contracted marriage *per verba de praesenti* before the ceremony in church. John Maides of Snitterfield testified that in 1585, before two witnesses, Alice Shaw of Hatton said to William Holder of Fulbrook, "I do confesse that I am your wief and have forsaken all my frendes for your sake, and I hope you will use me well," and gave him her hand, and that William "used the like words unto her in effect, and toke her by the hand, and kissed together." The consistory court at Worcester declared that they were therefore man and wife. So in 1621 William Ball promised marriage to his Ann and gave her a token, so that, John Trewman of Feckenham wrote to the vicar of Stratford, "they be man and wife before God and the world, although matrimony be not solemnized." Under common law, however, marriage solemnized by a clergyman was necessary to prove a wife's right to dower or a child's right to inherit.[5]

The entries of marriage licenses at Worcester name only one parish, nearly always the parish where the bride was living. The Shakespeare entry in the bishop's register suggests the possibility that Anne was then living at Temple Grafton, three and a half miles west of Shottery, but the bond describes her as of Stratford. A Puritan survey of Warwickshire ministers in 1586 called the vicar of Grafton, John Frith, "an old priest & Unsound in religion, he can neither prech nor read well, his chiefest trade is to cure hawkes y[t] are hurt or diseased, for which purpose manie doe usuallie repaire to him." Bishop Whitgift's officers had evidently kept an eye on him, for in 1580 they required him to give bond not to marry without license "any persons at any times prohibited by the ecclesiasticall lawes" and to marry no one at other times "without axinge the bannes in the churche thre Soundayes or holidayes solemly." This shows that a license might permit marriage even during Advent. If Shakespeare and Anne were not married at Temple Grafton, they could have been married at one of two chapels in the parish of Stratford, Bishopton just north of Shottery or Luddington to the south. The Bishopton register begins only in 1591 and bishop's transcripts of registers at Temple Grafton and Luddington not until 1612. The curate of Bishopton in 1587 was John Haines; the curate of Luddington, Thomas Hunt, was suspended in 1584. One of these men, or old John Frith, may have married Shakespeare and Anne Hathaway.[6]

Anne's father, Richard Hathaway, was probably the son of John Hathaway, who in 1556 held, by copy granted him in 1543, a house in Shottery, with a half-yardland, called "Hewland," a house and yardland late in the tenure of Thomas Perkyns, and a toft and half-yardland called "Hewlyns." A yardland or virgate varied in size from twenty to forty-six acres; Shakespeare's four yardlands in Old Stratford contained 107 acres.

A John Hathaway, archer, of Shottery, was on the muster-roll in 1536, a John was constable in 1548, and a John was assessed on an income of ten pounds in goods in the subsidy for 1549–50. Richard Hathaway was assessed on an income of four pounds in goods in the subsidy for 1566–67. His will named seven children living in 1581: Agnes and Catherine, not yet married; Margaret, under seventeen; Bartholomew, of age; and Thomas, John, and William, all under twenty. The Stratford registers record the baptism in 1563 of Catherine, daughter of Richard Hathaway alias Gardner; in 1569 of Thomas, son of Richard Hathaway; in 1572 of Margaret, daughter of "Gardner of Shotrey"; in 1574/5 of John, son of Richard Hathaway; and in 1578 of William, son of Richard Hathaway of Shottery. A Richard Hathaway was baptized in 1559, and the burial of Richard, son of Richard Hathaway alias Gardner, was entered in 1561 under both March 29 and April 1. Another Richard, son of Richard Hathaway alias Gardner, was baptized in 1561/2 and Joan, daughter of Richard Hathaway alias Gardner of Shottery, in 1566, but these two died before 1581. Agnes and Bartholomew, born before the registers begin in 1558, were probably children by an earlier wife of Richard.[7]

Richard Hathaway sued Robert Miles, brewer, for debt in 1563, and in 1566 John Shakespeare became his surety and was called on to pay debts of Richard Hathaway to John Page and Joan Biddle. Richard Hathewaye alias Gardner of Shottery owed money in 1578 to Roger Sadler, baker. In his will made September 1, 1581, Richard Hathway of Shottery, husbandman, left substantial legacies to his children: ten pounds to his youngest son William and ten marks each to Thomas, John, Agnes at the day of her marriage, Catherine at the day of her marriage, and Margaret at the age of seventeen. His eldest son Bartholomew was to have the use and profit of a half-yardland, but if Richard's wife Joan should deny Bartholomew this she was to pay him forty pounds. Richard wished that "Bartholemewe shalbe a guyde unto my saide wife in her husbandrie, And also a Comforte unto his Bretherne and Sisters to his power." Joan was executrix and residuary legatee, the supervisors of the will were "my Trustie ffryndes and neighboures Stephen Burman and ffowlke Sandels," and the witnesses included Sir William Gilbard, curate, Richard Burman, John Rychardson, and John Hemynge. His debts were to be paid and he was to be buried in the church or churchyard of Stratford, where his burial was recorded on September 7. Like Shakespeare's, his will was proved at London in the prerogative court of Canterbury, though most Shottery wills were proved at Stratford. His friend Fulk Sandells priced the goods in 1591 of Roger Burman, worth fifty-three pounds, and in 1594 of John Richardson, worth eighty-seven pounds and including six and a half score sheep.[8]

Richard Hathaway was mentioned by two Chancery witnesses at London in 1584. "Foulke Sandell" of Shottery, yeoman, aged thirty-three, testified on April 29 that he and other jurors at a manor court for Old Stratford presented certain land in Shottery as the Earl of Warwick's "upon the Report of one hathwaye alias Gardener," the earl's tenant, "the said gardener being then dead." Richard Burman of Shottery, husbandman, aged sixty, on May 1 "saith that by the report of one Ry. hathway alias Gardener deceassed, and of one Roger Burman," the jurors found that eleven butts of land within the fields of Shottery, abutting upon the moor, were the earl's as part of the "ferme grounde" of Old Stratford. Roger Burman had testified that "he heard his elders say so" and Richard Hathaway had "sayd he heard his father say the same." Roger Burman, said Sandells, had dwelt on the manor "by the space of fourescore yeres or verye nere." Another witness in 1584 was Stephen Burman of Stratford, yeoman, aged forty-six, the trusty friend of Richard Hathaway.[9]

Richard's widow Joan remained in Shottery, where she had two and a half yardlands in 1590 and a household of six in 1595, probably including her sons John and William and her shepherd Thomas Whittington. John Hathaway of Old Stratford was a soldier at musters in 1596 and 1599. His mother was buried in 1599 as "Jone Gardner de Shottrey." Richard in his will had acknowledged that he owed £4 6s. 8d. to Thomas Whittington his shepherd. When Whittington made his will on March 25, 1601, John and William Hathaway owed him about three pounds, besides £2 17s. left him by the will of their mother Joan. His estate was valued at fifty pounds. The most interesting bequest in his will gave "unto the poore people of Stratford 40s. that is in the hand of Anne Shaxspere, wyf unto Mr Wyllyam Shaxspere, and is due debt unto me, beyng payd to myne Executor by the sayd Wyllyam Shaxspere or his assigns."[10]

Anne Shakespeare's brother was described as Bartholomew Hathaway alias Garner of Tysoe, husbandman, in 1583, when he held the lease of a house in Ely Street. He married on November 25, 1581, Isabel Hancocks of Tredington, and had a son Richard (bailiff in 1626) and three children who were christened at Stratford: "Annys" in 1583/4 (Anne in her marriage entry and her father's will), John, and Edmund. He signed the register as churchwarden from 1605 to 1609. A farmer in Shottery, he appraised estates there in 1586 and 1608 and succeeded to his father's copyhold after the death of Joan in 1599. He was sued in the King's Bench in 1605/6 by Bartholomew Clarke, who also sued John Hathaway and others. In 1610 he bought for two hundred pounds Hewlands and the other property which he and his family had held since 1543 and which was owned by his descendants until 1838. In the subsidy of 1621 he was one of seven men taxed on land in Old Stratford. His will in 1621 left the property to his second son, John, with one hundred and twenty pounds to Edmund, and named as overseers John Hall, Shakespeare's son-in-law, and Stephen Burman the younger. He was buried at Stratford on October 20, 1624.[11]

William and Anne Shakespeare may have lived with his parents in Henley Street, for there is no record that they had a house of their own until Shakespeare bought New Place in 1597. By the time he came of age he was the father of three children. "Susanna daughter to William Shakspere" was christened on May 26, 1583, and the twins Hamnet and Judith on February 2, 1584/5. The name Susanna, from the Apocrypha, was fairly new in Stratford, first appearing in the register in 1574, but two girls were so christened in April, 1583, and Mr. Richard Woodward of Shottery had named two daughters Susanna and Judith. The twins were evidently named for Hamnet and Judith Sadler, a young couple in High Street. Sadler witnessed the will of Shakespeare, who left him money to buy a ring.[12]

CHAPTER VI

GENTLEMEN

AND PLAYERS

❖So far as is now known, Shakespeare lived in Stratford until about 1585, but by 1592 he was a player and poet in London. On these seven years the records are silent. Since it is possible that he may have taken service in a gentleman's household, we should know something of the chief gentlemen connected with Stratford; and since he became a player, we shall review the evidence for the touring companies which visited Stratford.

Traditions about Shakespeare's youth are late and contradictory. Since a tradition is a yarn, it is usually more or less twisted. Thomas Plume in 1657 or later set down one true fact about Shakespeare, that he was a glover's son, but the rest of this note reports a meeting between Sir John Mennis, born in 1599, and Shakespeare's father, who died in 1601. Mennis, who collected poems and anecdotes, may have borrowed the story from an earlier visitor to Stratford. Like Drayton and Jonson, he wrote verses printed in 1636 in *Annalia Dubrensia,* celebrating Robert Dover and the country sports on Cotswold.[1]

John Aubrey had asked questions at Stratford before 1681, when he wrote of Shakespeare that "his father was a Butcher, & I have been told heretofore by some of the neighbours, that when he was a boy he exercised his father's Trade, but when he kill'd a Calfe, he would doe it in a *high style,* & make a Speech." Since Shakespeare's father was not a butcher, the rest of the story is also doubtful, though entertainers sometimes acted out the "killing of a calf." Aubrey had better authority, William Beeston, for writing of Shakespeare that "He understood Latine pretty well: for he had been in his younger yeares a Schoolmaster in the Countrey." Beeston was "bred up a stage player" by his father Christopher Beeston, who acted with Shakespeare in *Every Man in His Humour* in 1598.[2]

An old parish clerk and sexton at Stratford, William Castle, born there in 1614, told a Mr. Dowdall in 1693 that Shakespeare "was formerly in this Towne bound apprentice to a butcher; but that he Run from his master to London, and there was Received Into the playhouse as a serviture . . . ." This varies and expands the tradition recorded by Aubrey.[3]

The story of Shakespeare's deer-stealing was first mentioned by Richard Davies between 1688 and 1708: "much given to all un-luckinesse in stealing venison & Rabbits particularly from S^r[*blank*] Lucy who had him oft whipt & sometimes Imprisoned & at last made Him fly his Native Country to his great Advancement. but His reveng was so great that he is his Justice Clodpate and calls him a great man & y^t in allusion to his name bore three lowses rampant for his Arms." Davies was referring to Justice Shallow in the first scene of *The Merry Wives of Windsor,* and this scene may have suggested the story. Aubrey would surely have set down the tale if he had ever heard it. Nicholas Rowe wrote in 1709, drawing on information gathered by Thomas Betterton in Warwickshire, that Shakespeare was prosecuted by Sir Thomas Lucy of Charlecote for robbing his park of deer, that he made a ballad upon Lucy, and that this redoubled the prosecution against him so that he was obliged to leave his business and family and shelter himself in London. William Oldys and Edward Capell later quoted an alleged "first stanza of that bitter ballad" learned before 1703 from "several old people at Stratford," who also said that the ballad against Sir Thomas "was stuck upon his park gate." The Sir Thomas Lucy who died in 1600 had no park in Warwickshire, though he had a coney warren, and the whole story seems to be a late invention.⁴

Betterton heard at Stratford, and told Rowe, that John Shakespeare "was a considerable Dealer in Wool," a statement which Dr. Hotson has proved true by records. He also heard that Shakespeare's wife "was the Daughter of one *Hathaway*, said to have been a substantial Yeoman in the Neighbourhood of *Stratford*." Relying in part on tradition and in part on inference, Rowe stated that Shakespeare's father "could give him no better Education than his own Employment. He had bred him, 'tis true, for some time at a Free-School, where 'tis probable he acquir'd that little *Latin* he was Master of: But the narrowness of his Circumstances, and the want of his assistance at Home, forc'd his Father to withdraw him from thence, and unhappily prevented his further Proficiency in that Language." Rowe could have inferred most of this from his knowledge that Stratford had a free school, that Shakespeare knew some Latin, and that he did not go on to a university. Betterton may possibly have heard at Stratford that Shakespeare attended the grammar school and that he was withdrawn to help his father at home.

Weighing the different traditions, we see that Plume was well-informed in calling Shakespeare's father a glover and Rowe in calling him a dealer in wool. Aubrey was not well-informed in calling him a butcher. The only evidence that Shakespeare was ever an apprentice comes from a very doubtful source, the parish clerk in 1693. The deer-stealing story was not mentioned by Aubrey or the parish clerk but was current in Stratford before 1703. Rowe believed that Shakespeare was withdrawn from school to work for his father, but this is hardly consistent with the tradition that he became a schoolmaster.

That Shakespeare "had been in his younger yeares a Schoolmaster in the Countrey" comes from a reliable informant, William Beeston. Elizabethan teachers of boys were sometimes hardly more than boys themselves. Simon Forman was nineteen (though he later claimed that he was under eighteen) and had served as apprentice for five years when in 1572 he began teaching for half a year and then "wente to Oxford for to get more lerninge." George Buck, who later licensed plays as master of the revels, became master of Chicester cathedral school in December, 1578, when he was only eighteen, since he was baptized on October 1, 1560. Henry Sturley was twenty and had studied at Oxford when in 1597 he became assistant master at Stratford. Shakespeare could have been a master or assistant master "in the Countrey" (anywhere outside London), or he could have been a private schoolmaster in a gentleman's household.[5]

Shakespeare might also have lived with some country gentleman who kept a company of players. A recent conjecture tries to identify him with one William Shakeshafte who in 1580 and 1581 served Alexander Houghton of Lea Hall in Lancashire. By his will in 1581 Houghton left all his musical instruments and "playe clothes" to his brother Thomas Houghton if Thomas should keep players, and if not, to Sir Thomas Hesketh, and he requested Hesketh "to be ffrendlye unto ffoke Gyllome and william Shakeshafte nowe dwellynge with me" and either take them to his service or help them to some good master. Fulk Gyllome probably came from Chester, where a Foulk Gillam became a freeman in 1596. Since dozens of Shakeshaftes lived in Lancashire and Cheshire, there is no real evidence to support the theory that William Shakeshafte was William Shakespeare. It is possible, however, that Shakespeare may have served some gentleman who lived nearer Stratford.[6]

The gentlemen most often mentioned in Stratford records during Elizabeth's reign were Sir Thomas Lucy of Charlecote and Sir Fulke Greville of Beauchamp's Court. Sir Thomas Lucy (1532–1600) had been tutored by John Foxe before he married at the age of fourteen Joyce Acton, aged twelve, who brought him rich estates at Sutton in Worcestershire. In 1555 "mr Luce" saw a play at Banbury, and "Sir Thomas Lucies players" received ten shillings at Coventry in the year ending in November, 1584. He built the great house at Charlecote, where Leicester knighted him in 1565 and Queen Elizabeth visited him in 1572, giving his daughter a jewel enameled with a butterfly between two daisies. In 1568 he was godfather to Thomas Sandys, son of the Bishop of Worcester, and in 1571 he entertained Thomas Ashton, Sidney's master at Shrewsbury school. His household book shows that he kept about forty servants and retainers at Charlecote or at Sutton, including Abraham Sturley and John Challoner, a tutor in languages for his son Thomas. As a member of parliament in 1571 he presented a petition for Puritan ministers, and on orders from the Privy Council in 1583 he arrested Edward Arden at Park Hall and searched the house of Edward Grant at Northbrooke. As a justice and deputy lieutenant he was often at Stratford, where the town gave him sack and claret at the Bear in 1581 and at the Swan in 1595 and 1597. He had keepers at Sutton Park and a "keeper of my coney warren" at Charlecote. Camden and other heralds attended his funeral, and his alabaster effigy in armor may still be seen in Charlecote church.[7]

The first Sir Thomas Lucy has often been confused with his son and grandson of the same name. Sir Thomas Lucy the second (1551–1605) had sixteen children by two heiresses, Dorothy Arnold of Gloucestershire and Constance Kingsmill of Hampshire. After his first marriage in 1573/4 he lived mainly in Gloucestershire, where he was sheriff in 1589. "Sir Thomas Lucye, of the county of Gloucester," was living in 1595 in Tower ward, London. In the year after he succeeded to Charlecote he was deputy lieutenant and sheriff of Warwickshire, and in 1604 the Stratford aldermen brought a gift of sturgeon "when they went to welcome Sir Tho. Lucie into the Countrie." He entertained them at Charlecote that Christmas, which proved to be his last. His will left to his son Thomas his best horse and "all my Frenche and Italian bookes." Sir Thomas the third (1585–1640) entered Lincoln's Inn in 1602, traveled in France with Sir Edward Herbert, and was mentioned in a letter by Donne and in a poem addressed to him by John Davies of Hereford. He brought a Star Chamber bill in 1610 against gentlemen who had stolen deer from his park at Sutton, and in 1618 he was licensed to impale a park at Charlecote. Strolling players arrested at Banbury in 1633 had acted at his house.

Besides serving in parliament between 1614 and 1640, he succeeded Lord Brooke as recorder of Stratford, in 1632 conferring with John Hall and sending the town a buck. A painting by Cornelius Janssen shows him at Charlecote with his wife, Alice Spencer, and seven of their fourteen children. His brother George Lucy of Oxford and Gray's Inn wrote verses in 1612 "To my friend, Mr Ben: Ionson. upon his Alchemist."[8]

Sir Fulke Greville of Beauchamp's Court near Alcester was often entertained at Stratford with the first Sir Thomas Lucy. He was recorder of the town from 1591 until his death in 1606, when his son the poet succeeded him in the office. Shakespeare could have seen him at Stratford in 1581, in 1583, and in 1584, when Greville and Lucy arbitrated a suit brought by Hamnet Sadler. In 1588 Greville sent horsemen to Tilbury and "gave Charge for the muskettes" at Stratford, staying with Richard Woodward at Shottery Manor. He invited Richard Quiney and other friends from Stratford to visit him during Christmas in 1601. He was then hoping that the queen would sell him Warwick Castle, "the ruins of a house," "the roof open to all weathers," so that soon "there will be nothing left but a name of Warwick," and he wrote Cecil that for his help "I will give you the finest high-flying tercel that ever you were master of." His son bought the estate from King James and saved the castle. After the Gunpowder Plot "yt was said that Sir Foulke Grevils howse was beseiged," but the old deputy lieutenant "raised the country" and was praised for his services by King James. Camden wrote that "the nobleness of his mind far surpasses that of his birth," and a history of the family in 1644 declared that "in his time no man did beare a greater sway in the Countie of Warwick than himselfe. He was evermore attended with a brave companie of gentlemen."[9]

Lodowick Greville of Milcote, on the Avon near Stratford, appears as "Mr. Grevill" in the Stratford records. In his many Star Chamber suits he signed his name "Lodowyk Grevill." The town gave him wine in 1579–80 and he gave the town a buck in 1582–83. After his marriage to Thomasine, daughter of Sir William

Petre, secretary of state, he began to build in 1567, but never finished, a great house called Mount Greville. In 1579 he was imprisoned for striking down Sir John Conway of Arrow in the streets of London. In the Armada year he sent as many horsemen to Tilbury as his cousin Sir Fulke. By this time he had accomplished the murder by strangling in bed of a tenant, Thomas Webbe of Drayton, Oxfordshire, and had caused one of his servants, impersonating Webbe and "dolefully groaning," to make a will in favor of Greville. His servant Thomas Brocke, "in his Cups at Stratford," boasted that it lay in his power to hang his master, after which Greville had him murdered by his fellow-murderer, Thomas Smith alias Barber, who was arrested and confessed the plot. After ten months in the Tower, Greville was convicted of Webbe's murder, stood mute in order to save his estates for his son Edward, and was pressed to death on November 14, 1589.[10]

When young Edward Greville once shot an arrow straight up and it fell and killed his elder brother, his father, Dugdale had heard, "made a jest of it, telling him that it was the best shoot he ever shot in his life." Edward became lord of Stratford after the death of the Earl of Warwick. A patent of 1590/91 to two London scriveners, Henry Best and John Wells, who conveyed their rights to Greville, brought him the lordship of the borough, with rents of ten pounds a year and the fees from the court leet, and the manor of Old Stratford, with rents of fifty-one pounds a year. He also presented the vicar and claimed the right of approving or rejecting the town's choice for bailiff. The chamberlains of Stratford paid in 1594 for the keeper's fee "at the eating of Mr. Grevilles bucke," for "a bankett at the Beare for Mr. Grevill," and "for peares and walnuttes at Mr. Grevills returne from Scottlande." This was the year of Prince Henry's christening at Stirling. When Greville was sheriff the next year the town gave him sack at the Swan with Sir Thomas Lucy and Lady Lucy. His London residence in 1595 was in Bread Street ward and in 1600 in St. Giles in the Fields. Essex wrote him in 1596 to aid Sir Christopher Blount in levying soldiers for the expedition to Cadiz and named Greville as one of his

sureties to the queen for provisions. In November Greville and
Lucy held musters at Stratford, and in 1597 the town entertained
him at Mr. Quiney's and at the Swan. Essex knighted him at the
Azores in October, 1597, with the Earl of Southampton. Sturley
wrote of him in November as Sir Edward. Next year the town
provided wine and cakes "when my Lady Grevell cam to see our
sport." She was Joan, daughter of Sir Thomas Bromley, lord
chancellor, and her husband and her brother were commissioners
in 1599 for finding lands and goods of recusants. The disputes between Greville and the members of the corporation will be discussed
later, but they gave him sack and claret in 1602 and 1614 and con-
sulted him in 1609 about renewing their charter. Though he repre-
sented the shire in parliament in 1593 and 1604, his speculations
under James I ended in the loss of all his estates by 1622. Richard
Lane in 1613 bade his executor sue Greville on a bond for a
thousand pounds, Anthony Nash sued him in 1615, and a debt by
Greville to Richard Quiney's son Adrian was described in 1617 as
"uncertain to be got."[11]

The lord of the manor of Shottery in Stratford was Francis
Smith (1522–1605) of Wootton Wawen, son of Sir John Smith, a
baron of the Exchequer under Henry VIII, and Dame Agnes Smith,
daughter and coheiress of John Harewell of Wootton. He married his first wife in 1537 and served as sheriff of Warwickshire in
1566. Though he was a Catholic in 1564, Sir Fulke Greville and
Sir Thomas Lucy certified in 1586 that he was a good subject and
went to church, and he contributed to defense against the Armada.
His grandson reported at Rome in 1600, "My father and grandfather are schismatics." The Earl of Warwick claimed Baldon Hill
("Balgandun" in a Saxon charter before 709), which Smith had
granted to Richard Woodward as part of the farm of Shottery.
Stephen Burman and other Chancery witnesses in 1584 quoted high
words that passed between Mr. Smith and the Earl's officers and
Richard and Roger Burman in the parlor of John Smith, vintner,
at Stratford. Francis Smith reclines in alabaster in the church of
Wootton Wawen, "before the place where I have usuallye satt,"

with his arms of four peacocks for Smith and three hares' heads for Harewell.[12]

John Somerville of Edstone in Wootton Wawen, a Catholic who had studied at Oxford, inherited his father's estates in 1578, when he was eighteen, and married Margaret, daughter of Edward Arden of Park Hall. He invested money with the Quineys on October 14, 1583. Earlier that year he had talked at Coventry with his friend Henry Goodere about Mary Queen of Scots. On October 25 he set out from Edstone for London, saying, "I will go up to the Court and shoot the Queen through with a pistol." Arrested and convicted of treason, he was found strangled in his cell at Newgate the day before he was to have been put to death.[13]

Sir William Catesby (1547–1598) was described as of Stratford when he became sheriff of the county in 1577, and the town gave him wine in 1580. His house, Bushwood or Lapworth Hall, belonged to the parish and manor of Stratford, though it stood in Lapworth, twelve miles to the north. He bought Shottery Meadow in 1581 and sold Bishopton manor in 1583. A recusant in 1580, he offered in 1585 to compound for his fines by paying one hundred pounds of his five hundred a year. He was imprisoned in the Fleet and tried in Star Chamber in 1581 for refusing to say whether or not Edmund Campion had been in his house. In 1588 he was a prisoner at Ely and in 1593 he was allowed to visit Bath for his health. He was living at Milcote in 1597 with Sir Edward Greville, "his good friend and near kinsman," who after his death bought a manor in Lapworth from Catesby's son Robert, the Gunpowder conspirator. His ancestor, the Catesby of *Richard III*, is often called by editors "Sir William," but his will made shortly before his beheading shows that he was "William Catesby, Esquire."[14]

Edward Aglionby (also spelled at Stratford "Egleby," "eglinbe," "Edglumbe") was recorder of Stratford from 1576 to 1586, as he was of Warwick from 1572 to 1587. Born at Carlisle in 1520, he studied at Eton under Nicholas Udall. Taking the degree of M.A. at Cambridge, he wrote Latin poems and published at

Worcester in 1550 a translation of Gribaldi's *Epistle Concerning the Judgment of God* on Francis Spira. He fought the Scots at Solway Moss in 1542 and served as paymaster for the Earl of Warwick in the Northern Rising of 1569. Edward Aglionby of Temple Balsall and Henry Higford of Solihull (later steward of Stratford and a creditor of John Shakespeare) bought many church lands in 1553, including lordships of Balsall commandery and a house in Henley Street. Aglionby served in parliament for Carlisle in 1553 and for Warwick in 1571. When he welcomed Queen Elizabeth to Warwick in 1572 with an oration, "she called Mr. Aglionby to her, and offred her hand to him to kisse, withall smyling, said, 'Come hither, little Recorder. It was told me that yowe wold be afraid to look upon me, or to speak boldly; but you were not so fraid of me as I was of youe.' " The townsmen of Stratford entertained him for supper at the Bear in 1577 and for dinner in 1583.[15]

Shakespeare could have seen other guests of the town during these years. Ambrose, Earl of Warwick, present at the "great leet" for his manors of Stratford and Old Stratford, was entertained at the Swan in 1582 and was given wine in 1584. The town sent him an ox as a gift in each of these years. Sack and claret were furnished at the Bear in April, 1583, for Sir Fulke Greville, George Digby of Coleshill, and Thomas Dabridgecourt of Solihull, and in the same year for the sheriff, John Harrington of Combe Abbey. At the Swan in 1586 the town entertained the Puritan leader Thomas Cartwright from Warwick with Job Throckmorton, who in 1589 set up a printing press for Martin Marprelate in his house at Haseley. By that time Shakespeare was probably in London.[16]

The first professional actors known to have played at Stratford came in 1569, when John Shakespeare was bailiff. He approved a reward of nine shillings to the Queen's players and one of twelve-pence to the Earl of Worcester's players. These were for official performances in the gild hall, where the players might also gather money, as they did at later performances in an innyard. At Warwick the Queen's men had pleased "Master Baily and his Brethren," who watched them play twice in 1566 at the Maiden Head and again in 1568 in the School House. They were at Bristol in August, 1569. Worcester's men visited Stratford probably on their way from Nottingham, where they played in August, to Bristol, where they played in September, 1569.[17]

The Earl of Leicester's men, led by James Burbage, were at Stratford in 1573, probably in September on their way from Nottingham to Bristol. "Master Bayly," Roger Sadler, paid their reward and was repaid by the chamberlains. The Earl of Warwick's men, wearing his badge of the bear and ragged staff and probably led by John and Laurence Dutton, came in 1574–75, perhaps in the summer of 1575 when the queen visited Kenilworth and Warwick. They received a generous reward of seventeen shillings, since their master was lord of Stratford. A payment to the Earl of Worcester's men in the accounts for the same year follows an entry referring to January 4, 1575/6. In 1576–77 Leicester's players were given fifteen shillings and Worcester's only three shillings fourpence. At Bristol in October, 1577, Leicester's company performed a play called *Myngo*.[18]

Seven different companies played at Stratford between 1579 and 1584. Lord Strange's men were paid on February 11, 1578/9, "at the commaundment of Mr Baliffe," Thomas Barber of the Bear Inn. They were at Nottingham in 1578 and at Coventry in 1578–79. The Countess of Essex's players, who were also at Coventry, came to Stratford probably in August, 1579. The Earl of Derby's players acted there in 1580, probably before October. In 1580–81 Stratford saw Worcester's men and Lord Berkeley's men, who at Bristol in 1578 had acted a play called *What Mischief Worketh in the Mind of Man*. Worcester's came also in 1581–82, and the next year Lord Berkeley's and Lord Chandos's companies, both of which were at Gloucester in November, 1582. Players of the Earls of Oxford, Worcester, and Essex came to Stratford during 1583–84. Worcester's men, who included Robert Browne and the seventeen-year-old Edward Alleyn, were forbidden to act at Leicester on March 6, 1583/4, but they "went with their drums & trumppytts

thorowe the towne, in contempt of Mr Mayor," and were finally
allowed to play that night at their inn. They also acted during
1583–84 at Gloucester and Coventry, while Essex's men were visiting the same towns and Leicester, Shrewsbury, Ludlow, and Bristol. A company not named in the records was at Stratford in 1585–
86.[19]

The best year for plays at Stratford during Elizabeth's reign was
1587. Five companies appear in the accounts from December, 1586,
to December, 1587: the players of the Queen, of Essex, of Leicester, "another Companye," and Lord Stafford's men. The town
also paid "for mendinge of a forme that was broken by the quenes
players." Leicester's men acted at Coventry in July and on August
1, and the Queen's men acted there twice in September. The bailiff
of Stratford, Thomas Barber of the Bear, gave the Queen's men
twenty shillings, the largest reward players had ever received at
Stratford. They wore scarlet coats as servants of the Queen, who
had ordered them chosen in 1583 from the best actors in London,
including Richard Tarlton.[20]

Malone suggested that Shakespeare may have joined Leicester's
or Warwick's or the Queen's men when they played at Stratford,
and Pollard thought that he may have joined the Queen's men at
Stratford in 1586 or 1587. These are only conjectures, but I have
discovered evidence that the Queen's men were lacking one actor
in the summer of 1587, for William Knell had just been killed by
his fellow John Towne. A coroner's inquest at Thame in Oxfordshire, viewing the body of Knell, reported that between nine and
ten at night on June 13, 1587, Knell came into a close called White
Hound in Thame and assaulted with his sword John Towne of
Shoreditch, yeoman. Fearing for his life, Towne withdrew to a
mound beyond which he could neither cross nor descend without
danger, and when Knell continued his assault maliciously and
furiously, Towne drew his sword and thrust it into the throat of
Knell, who died half an hour after. Since the jury found that
Towne struck in self-defense, he was pardoned by the Queen on
August 15. William Knell had married Rebecca Edwards in

1585/6 at St. Mary, Aldermanbury, London, and his widow married there in 1587/8 John Heminge, who became Shakespeare's close friend. Knell was praised as an actor by Nashe and Heywood; according to *Tarlton's Jests,* he had played Prince Henry in a play which was probably *The Famous Victories of Henry the Fifth.* If so, *The Famous Victories,* usually dated before the death of Tarlton in 1588, can now be dated before the death of Knell in 1587.[21]

The officials of Stratford made only one contribution for a performance by their own townsmen, in 1583 when they paid thirteen shillings fourpence "to Davi Jones and his companye for his pastyme at whitsontyde." Davy Jones had married in 1577 Elizabeth, daughter of Adrian Quiney, and after her death two years later he married Frances Hathaway. Shakespeare may have been one of the young men who took part in this pastime

At Pentecost,
When all our pageants of delight were played.[22]

CHAPTER VII

SHAKESPEARE

AT NEW PLACE

❖After the baptism of Hamnet and Judith on February 2, 1584/5, the next record of Shakespeare's family is the burial of Hamnet on August 11, 1596. Anne Shakespeare and the children probably remained in Stratford while Shakespeare was establishing himself in London. As soon as he could afford it, he helped his father to secure a coat of arms and provided for his family one of the best houses in Stratford.

According to a manuscript at the College of Arms, John Shakespeare showed the heralds in 1596 a "patierne" of a coat of arms made "xx yeares past" under the hand of Robert Cook, Clarencieux king of arms from 1567 to 1592. The heralds' notes added that John was a justice of peace and bailiff of Stratford "xv or xvi years past" (an error for "xxvii") and "That he hathe Landes & tenementes. Of good wealth & Substance/500¹¹." The first draft of the grant mentioned that John married "Mary daughter & one of the heyres of Robert Arden of Wilmcote in the said Counte gentleman." On October 20, 1596, "William Dethick Garter principall king of Arms" granted a coat of arms and crest to John Shakespeare, "being solicited and by credible report informed" that his "parentes & late Grandfather for his faithfull & valeant service [were] advaunced & rewarded by the most Prudent Prince King Henry the seventh of famous memorie, sythence whiche tyme they have continewed in those partes being of good reputacion & credit, & that the said John hathe maryed the daughter & one of the heyres of Robert Arden of Wilmcote in the said Counte esquire." The word "Grandfather" in this second draft of the grant was written above the word "antecessors" and "gent' " was crossed out and replaced by "esquire." Since no evidence has been found that any Shakespeare was rewarded by Henry VII, this story may have been invented, unless it referred to an ancestor of another surname now unknown, such as John's mother's father. The heralds were unreliable in estimating John's wealth and in calling Robert Arden gentleman and esquire, when he was described during his lifetime as husbandman.[1]

At all events, John Shakespeare was clearly entitled to a grant of arms, since he had served as bailiff of Stratford. Dethick assigned to him and his posterity these arms: "Gould. on A Bend Sables. a Speare of the first steeled argent. And for his Creast or Cognizaunce a falcon. his winges displayed Argent. standing on a wrethe of his Coullors. supporting a Speare Gould. steeled as aforesaid sett uppon a helmett with mantelles & tasselles." By this grant he became officially John Shakespeare, gentleman, though he was still called yeoman in his deed to George Badger in 1596/7. The arms and crest appear on Shakespeare's monument, and the arms were used, impaled with those of Hall, by Susanna and John Hall. Both drafts of the grant add a motto, "non sanz droict."[2]

John Shakespeare, or his son William acting for him, later asked the heralds to confirm his right to bear the arms of Arden impaled with his own. This confirmation may not have been completed, for the Shakespeare and Arden arms have not been found together except in a draft at the College of Arms. The draft, which left a blank for the day and month, is dated in the forty-second year of Elizabeth's reign, "1599," or between November 17, 1599, and March 24, 1599/1600. By its terms William Dethick, Garter king of arms, and William Camden, Clarencieux, granted and confirmed to John Shakespeare and to his posterity the right to bear his arms, described as in 1596, either single or impaled with the arms of Arden. A herald began to draw in the margin of the draft the arms of Arden of Park Hall but replaced these with arms borne by other Arden families: "Gules, three cross crosselets fitchées and a chief or, with a martlet for difference." These arms prove nothing about the actual descent of Robert Arden, for similar arms were borne by the Ardens of Cheshire, by their descendant William of Bedfordshire, and, if Fuller was not mistaken, by the second son of Thomas of Park Hall, Simon, sheriff of Warwickshire in 1569. The writer of the draft was wrong in putting "WellingCote" for "Wilmcote" and in saying that the arms produced by John Shakespeare had been assigned to him while he was bailiff. The draft changed "parent and Antecessor" by interlining to make it read "parent great Grandfather and late Antecessor." It improved on the drafts of 1596 by stating more specifically that Henry VII had rewarded this ancestor with lands and tenements in Warwickshire. John Shakespeare died in 1601, and his son's monument has only the Shakespeare arms.[3]

Dethick was charged in 1602 by his enemy Ralph Brooke, York herald, with granting to the Shakespeares arms which "Usurpe the Coate of the Lo. Mauley," a bend sable. Dethick answered that "the Speare on the Bend. is a patible difference. And the man was A magestrat in Stratford upon Avon. A Justice of peace. he maryed A daughter and heyre of Ardern. and was of good substance and habelite." Brooke's criticism was baseless, for Lord Mauley had no monopoly on a bend sable. Richard Quiney had a seal with a bend sable in 1591 and sealed his letter to Shakespeare in 1598 with his arms, "Or, on a bend sable, three trefoils slipped argent."[4]

New Place, Shakespeare's home in Stratford from 1597 until his death, was a house with a frontage of more than sixty feet on Chapel Street, a depth of about seventy feet along Chapel Lane, and a height of twenty-eight feet at the northern gable. Sir Hugh Clopton, lord mayor of London in 1491, at his death in 1496 left "my grete house in Stratford upon Avon" to William Clopton. Adrian Quiney the first was living at "the Newe Place" in 1532,

New Place and the Chapel in the Eighteenth Century

The College and the Church

but he died the next year. John Leland, visiting Stratford about 1540, learned that Sir Hugh had rebuilt the "right goodly chappell, in a fayre street towardes the south ende of the towne," and had "builded also by the north syde of this chappell a praty howse of brike and tymbar." William Clopton the second leased New Place in 1543 to Dr. Thomas Bentley, physician to Henry VIII and former president of the College of Physicians. When Bentley died in 1549, Clopton declared in Chancery that he "hath lefte the said manour place in great ruyne and decay and unrepayryd." William Bott was occupying the house at Clopton's death in 1560.[5]

Bott secured title to New Place in 1563 from the young heir, the third William Clopton of Clopton (1538–1592). Clopton had been selling or mortgaging lands to pay his father's legacies to his four sisters and to travel in Italy. He testified in Star Chamber in 1564 that Bott, acting as his agent while he was in Italy, had kept the rents received and had forged a deed concerning his lands. Soon after, he brought a Chancery suit against William Bott, late of Stratford on Avon, gentleman, for recovery of deeds and jewels. Bott acknowledged that he had evidences belonging to Clopton but declared that he had delivered to Lodowick Greville of Milcote, to redeliver to Clopton, bonds dated in 1564 by which Greville promised to pay Clopton one hundred pounds and forty pounds, and a recognizance by Greville in two thousand pounds; an indenture of defeasance to Clopton by Thomas Sackville, esquire, and another by Ralph Sheldon of Beoley; and deeds made to Clopton's father. Bott had also received from Greville a gold ring with five sparks of diamonds and from Greville through Richard Stoneley "certyn Juelles for to lay to gaydge for a certyn somme of money to be Conveyed by exchange over the sea into the partyes of Italy videlicet one Booke of golde two bracelettes of golde one Ryng of golde with a tabull dyamond, and one Ryng of golde with a Rock Ruby." Clopton had named his first son Lodowick in 1561, and his deed of covenant to Bott and John Goodale in 1563 was witnessed by Greville, William Porter, and Thomas Webbe. Greville was later sued in Star Chamber and

Chancery for conspiring to convey Clopton's lands to William Porter by a false deed dated in 1563/4, and Bott also sued Greville in Star Chamber.[6]

In a suit for slander in 1560, Bott declared that he had lived since childhood as a man of great honesty and credit among men both honorable and venerable in the counties of Stafford, Warwick, Worcester, and Northampton, but that he had lost "magna ineffabilia lucra" from yearly gifts, fees, and rewards since Richard Symons (deputy steward of Stratford) charged him with dishonesty in taking money to be of counsel with one Holwey and then making an opponent's plea against Holwey. He brought a similar suit in 1563, declaring that Roland Wheler said to him, at the Swan in Stratford: "Wylliam Bott thou art a false harlott a false vyllayne & a Rebellyon and I wyll make the to be sett on the pyllory." Wheler answered that Bott had first called him "a vyllayn & a Rowge." Bott's son-in-law charged in Star Chamber in 1564 that Bott had been "openly detected of divers great and notorious crimes, as namely felony, adultery, whoredom, falsehood, and forging." "Lett every man beeware of hyme," a witness warned, "for he is counted the craftieste marchant in all our contrey . . . and it is said that if botte had hade his Right he had been hanged longe ago."[7]

Bott was expelled from his office of alderman in 1565 for saying "that ther was never a honest man of the Councell or the body of the corporacyon of Stratford." In 1567 he sold New Place for forty pounds to William Underhill of the Inner Temple, clerk of assizes at Warwick, promising assurance by "one Raffe Botte," commonly called his son and heir apparent. Underhill also leased the tithes of Little Wilmcote in the parish of Stratford from the council, which gave him a dinner at the Swan. He was described in Star Chamber as "a verey good man," but his son and heir William was called by Stephen Burman "a subtle, covetous, and crafty man." The younger William, fourteen at his father's death in 1569/70, became ward to Sir Christopher Hatton, whose sister Dorothy was second wife of the elder William. William the younger and his wife Mary, who were first cousins by father and by mother, lived both at New Place and at Idlicote. Two sons were christened at Idlicote, Fulke in 1579 and Simon in 1589, and four children at Stratford, Dorothy in 1580, Elizabeth in 1585, a daughter Valentine three days after St. Valentine's day in 1587, and William in 1588. Though he was imprisoned for recusancy before 1579 and indicted before 1592, Underhill held the profitable office of escheator for Warwickshire and Leicestershire in 1587. Next year he entertained at New Place the recorder, Mr. James Dyer. The town of Stratford was suing him for tithe-rent in 1597, when he sold New Place. He died of poison at Fillongley on July 7, 1597, and his son Fulke was executed at Warwick in 1598/9 for murdering his father. The second son, Hercules, born on June 6, 1581, secured a grant of the forfeited estates on coming of age in 1602 and confirmed the sale of New Place to Shakespeare.[8]

Shakespeare paid William Underhill sixty pounds, if the fine is right, for the house with two barns and two gardens. He probably paid a small sum to Hercules Underhill to clear the title, though the fine levied in Michaelmas term, 1602, gave the nominal purchase-price as again sixty pounds. It also mentioned two orchards. For each fine the crown was entitled to one-fourth of the yearly value of the property. Shakespeare may have repaired the house, since a "m^r Shaxspere," either he or his father, sold the town a load of stone in 1598.[9]

The fifteenth-century house in which Shakespeare lived was pulled down by Sir John Clopton before 1702; the new house which Sir John built was pulled down by Francis Gastrell in 1759. Two descriptions survive of New Place as it looked at the end of the seventeenth century. George Vertue, engraver and antiquary, visited Stratford in 1737 and talked with Shakespeare Hart, glazier, born in 1670 and descended from Shakespeare's sister. Vertue made a pen-and-ink drawing, first published in 1952, "This Something by memory and ye description of Shakespears House," probably as described by Hart. The drawing shows a handsome three-story house with five gables. Vertue added: "This the outward appearance towards the Street. the gate and entrance, (at the Corner of chappel lane) . . . besides this front or outward gate there was before the House itself (that Shakespear livd in.) within a little court yard. grass growing there—before the real dwelling house. this outside being only a long gallery &c and for servants." These notes refer, not to the sketch of the house, but to a second drawing which shows the gate and a building on either side of the court in front of the house. A later description confirms this evidence that Shakespeare's main house stood well back from Chapel Street. Old Richard Grimmitt, born in 1683, remembered in 1767 that "He in his youth had been a playfellow with Edwd Clopton Senr eldest son of Sr John Clopton Kn^t. & had been often with him in ye Great House near ye Chapel in Stratford, call'd New-place: that to ye best of his remembrance there was a brick Wall next ye Street, with a kind of porch at that end of it next ye chapel; when they cross'd a small kind of Green Court before they enter'd ye House which was bearing to ye left, & fronted with brick, with plain windows Consisting of common panes of Glass set in lead, as at this time."[10]

The garden at New Place is first mentioned in 1563, and two years later Bott sued his neighbor Richard Sponer, painter, for taking twelve pieces of timber from "le barne yarde" near "le newe place gardyn" in "Dede Lane" (Chapel Lane). A second garden, the next land to the east in Chapel Lane, had belonged to Pinley Priory, dissolved in 1536, and was later owned by "m^r William shaxpeare." Orchards and gardens at New Place are mentioned in the wills of Thomas Nash in 1642 and of Lady Bernard in 1670. The "Great Garden . . . which formerly did belong to New Place" contained three-quarters of an acre in 1706. A mulberry tree in the garden, with a stock of six inches in diameter, was cut down in 1758, and the tradition that Shakespeare had planted the tree was affirmed in 1760 by the Stratford council and later by Hugh Taylor (1702–1788), an alderman of Warwick who had lived when a boy in the next house to New Place.[11]

The vines at New Place, probably grapevines, attracted the interest of Sir Thomas Temple, baronet (1567–1637). In 1631 Temple wrote this letter to one of his men:

Harry Rose, theese are to will yow to ride to Stratforde upon Avon at your next opportunity & to desire Mr Hall Phiscon from me to desire him to suffer Harry Rose, or any better in skill, to gather some few budes y^t is 2 or 3 of the fairest of those budes on some few shutes of the last yeares vines. His house is neare to the house of my brother Peter Temples wife, to whom I would have yow putt her in minde to request the same Mr Hall (which she promised to me), to gratifie me with some such shutes of his vine, which my sister commended much to me . . .

Temple gave Rose directions how to plant the "vine settes" at Dassett Court orchard in Warwickshire and at Wolverton in Buckinghamshire, where Temple lived from 1630 to 1637. He mentioned the same vine in other letters. His brother Peter had been declared a lunatic in 1619, but Peter's son, Mr. Peter Temple, had five children christened at Stratford between 1631 and 1637 and five children buried there in 1635 and 1636. "My brother Peter Temples wife," Mrs. Katherine Temple, lived before 1640 across the street from New Place, in the house still standing at the corner of Chapel Street and Scholars' Lane which by 1662 had become the Falcon Inn.[12]

Shakespeare probably settled his family at New Place during 1597, for he was a householder in Chapel Street ward by February 4, 1597/8. A survey of grain and malt in Stratford on that date lists Shakespeare as owning ten quarters of malt, or eighty bushels. This was a normal supply for household use; the schoolmaster, Mr. Aspinall, had eleven quarters, and the vicar, Mr. Byfield, had six of his own and four of his sister's. William Harrison, rector of Radwinter, gave the best contemporary description of household brewing, telling how his wife and her maidservants brewed once a month. Mrs. Shakespeare no doubt looked after the brewing at New Place, and her daughters were soon old enough to help. Twenty bushels of malt belonging to Shakespeare were sold by some member of his household, at different times between March and May, 1604, to his neighbor Philip Rogers, who also borrowed two shillings from Shakespeare or his family at Stratford on June 25. Since Rogers paid only six shillings of his debt, Shakespeare eventually, at an unspecified date, took the usual proceedings in the court of record to secure his money, employing William Tetherton as attorney. Philip Rogers, apothecary, who sold drugs and tobacco, was licensed to sell ale in 1603 and later, in Chapel Street in 1606 and in High Street in 1608. Two clergymen also had to sue him to collect their debts, while in 1604 he sued Valentine Palmes for unlawfully detaining a book which he valued at ten shillings twopence, *Certaine Workes of Chirurgerie* by Thomas Gale.[13]

In 1602 Shakespeare acquired the copyhold of a cottage on the south side of Chapel Lane, across from the garden of New Place, perhaps to house a gardener or other servant. Walter Getley surrendered this cottage, held of Rowington manor, to Shakespeare's use on September 28, 1602. A survey in 1604 records that Shakespeare held a cottage and a garden of a quarter-acre. His daughter Susanna Hall was admitted tenant in 1617.[14]

As soon as Shakespeare had a house of his own, he began to think about buying land near Stratford. Adrian Quiney told Abraham Sturley, and Sturley wrote to Richard Quiney on January 24, 1597/8, "that our countriman m^r Shaksper is willinge to disburse some monei upon some od yardeland or other att Shottreie or neare about us; he thinketh it a very fitt patterne to move him to deale in the matter of our Tithes. By the instruccions u can geve him theareof, and by the frendes he can make therefore, we thinke it a faire marke for him to shoote att, and not unpossible to hitt. It obtained would advance him in deede, and would do us muche good." Shakespeare did not draw his bow at a venture, but in 1602 he bought land in Old Stratford and in 1605 a lease of tithes.[15]

The only known letter addressed to Shakespeare was preserved in the Stratford archives because the writer, Richard Quiney, died in office as bailiff in 1602. Quiney was born before 1557, when his father Adrian married a second wife. Chosen alderman in 1588 and bailiff in 1592, he went to London on town affairs in 1593,

1595, and in every year from 1597 through 1601. When he wrote to Shakespeare on October 25, 1598, he was petitioning for a more favorable charter and for relief from taxes because the town was suffering from declining trade and from fires in 1594 and 1595. He succeeded in gaining for Stratford, in January, 1599, remission of all the taxes and subsidies granted by the last parliament.[16]

Quiney wrote to Shakespeare, from the Bell Inn near St. Paul's:

Loveinge Contreyman, I am bold of yow as of a ffrende, craveinge yowr helpe with xxx[11] uppon m[r] Bushells & my securytee or m[r] Myttons with me. m[r] Rosswell is nott come to London as yeate & I have especiall cawse. Yow shall ffrende me muche in helpeing me out of all the debettes I owe in London I thancke god & muche quiet my mynde which wolde nott be indebted. I am nowe towardes the Cowrte in hope of answer for the dispatche of my Buysenes. Yow shall nether loase creddytt nor money by me the Lorde wyllinge & nowe butt perswade yowr selfe soe as I hope & yow shall nott need to feare butt with all hartie thanckefullnes I wyll holde my tyme & content yowr ffrende & yf we Bargaine farther yow shalbe the paiem*aste*r yowr selfe. My tyme biddes me hasten to an ende & soe I committ thys yowr care & hope of yowr helpe. I feare I shall nott be backe thys night ffrom the Cowrte. Haste. The Lorde be with yow & with us all amen. ffrom the Bell in Carter Lane the 25 october 1598.
Yowrs in all kyndenes
Ryc. Quyney.

He endorsed the letter "To my Loveinge good ffrend & contreyman m[r] w[m] Shackespere de*live*r thees." The letter seems not to have been delivered, since it was found among Quiney's papers.[17]

Quiney needed money for the four months he spent in London urging the queen's officers to approve the petition from Stratford. He was counting on financial help from Sir Edward Greville, lord of the manor, and it was Greville's kinsmen, Bushell and Mytton, whom he offered as sureties for his loan from Shakespeare. Richard Mytton, gentleman, "servant" or officer to his cousin Sir Edward, acted for him in 1590–91 when Greville bought the manors of Stratford and Old Stratford. Peter Roswell was another gentleman in the service of Greville. "M[r] Bushell" may have been either

Thomas Bushell, esquire, of Broad Marston in the parish of Pebworth, Gloucestershire, or his son and heir Thomas. The Bishop of Gloucester described the elder Thomas in 1577 as the richest recusant in his diocese, worth five hundred pounds a year in lands and goods. When Quiney and William Parsons wrote to Greville in 1593 asking his consent in the election for bailiff, they sent the letter to Mr. William Sawnders, attendant on the worshipful Mr. Thomas Bushell at Marston. Mr. Bushell was mentioned in 1602 in the will of Joyce Hobday, widow of a Stratford glover. Thomas the elder married twice, had seventeen children, and died in 1615. His daughter Elinor married Quiney's son Adrian in 1613, and his son Henry married Mary Lane of Stratford in 1609. His son Thomas, aged fifteen when he entered Oxford in 1582, married as his first wife Margaret, sister of Sir Edward Greville. Bridges, a son by his second wife, was christened at Pebworth in 1607, but Thomas the younger was living at Packwood two years later and sold Broad Marston manor in 1622. A third Thomas Bushell (1594–1674), "much loved" by Bacon, called himself "the Superlative Prodigall" in *The First Part of Youths Errors* (1628) and became an expert on silver mines and on the art of running into debt.[18]

Edward Greville, born about 1565, had inherited Milcote on the execution of his father Lodowick for murder in 1589. He refused his consent to the election of Quiney as bailiff in 1592, but gave it at the request of the recorder, his cousin Sir Fulke Greville. The corporation entertained him for dinner at Quiney's house in 1596/7, with wine and sugar sent by the bailiff, Sturley. At Milcote on November 3, 1597, the aldermen asked him to support their petition for a new charter. Sturley wrote to Quiney that Sir Edward "gave his allowance and liking thereof, and affied unto us his best endeavour, so that his rights be preserved," and that "Sir Edward saith we shall not be at any fault for money for prosecuting the cause, for himself will procure it and lay it down for us for the time." Greville proposed Quiney as the fittest man "for the following of the cause and to attend him in the matter," and at his suggestion the corporation allowed Quiney two shillings a day. "If you can firmly make the good knight sure to pleasure our Corporation," Sturley wrote, "besides that ordinary allowance for your diet you shall have £20 for recompence."[19]

In his letter mentioning Shakespeare on January 24, 1597/8, Sturley asked Quiney especially that "theare might [be] bi Sir Ed. Grev. some means made to the Knightes of the Parliament for an ease and discharge of such taxes and subsedies wherewith our towne is like to be charged, and I assure u I am in great feare and doubte bi no meanes hable to paie. Sir Ed. Gre. is gonne to Brestowe and from thence to Lond. as I heare, who verie well knoweth our estates and wil be willinge to do us ani good." The knights for Warwickshire in this parliament, which ended its session on February 9, were Fulke Greville (the poet) and William Combe of Warwick, as Fulke Greville and Edward Greville had been in 1593. The corporation voted on September 27, 1598, that Quiney should ride to London about the suit to Sir John Fortescue, chancellor of the Exchequer, for discharging of the tax and subsidy. He had been in London for several weeks when he wrote to Shakespeare on October 25. Sturley on November 4 answered a letter from Quiney written on October 25 which imported, wrote Sturley, "that our countriman m^r Wm Shak. would procure us monei: which I will like of as I shall heare when wheare & howe: and I prai let not go that occasion if it mai sort to ani indifferent condicions. Allso that if monei might be had for 30 or 40[1] a lease &c. might be procured." Sturley quoted Quiney as having written on November 1 that if he had "more monei presente much might be done to obtaine our Charter enlargd, ij. faires more, with tole of corne, bestes, and sheepe, and a matter of more valewe then all that." Sturley thought that this matter might be "the rest of the tithes and the College houses and landes in our towne." He suggested offering half to Sir Edward, fearing lest "he shall thinke it to good for us and procure it for himselfe, as he served us the last time." This refers to what had happened after the Earl of Warwick died in 1590, when the town petitioned Burghley for the right to name the vicar and schoolmaster and other privileges but Greville bought the lordship for himself. Sturley's allusion probably explains why Greville took out the patent in the names of Best and Wells, for Sir Anthony Ashley described Best as "a scrivener within Temple Bar, that deals in many matters for my L. Essex" through Sir Gelly Merrick, especially in "causes that he would not be known of."[20]

Adrian Quiney wrote to his son Richard on October 29 and again perhaps the next day, since the bearer of the letter, the bailiff, was expected to reach London on November 1. In his second letter the old mercer advised his son "to bye some such warys as yow may selle presentlye with profet. yff yow bargen with W^m sha . . [so in the MS] or Receave money ther or brynge your money home yow maye see howe knite stockynges be sold ther ys gret byinge of them at Aysshom. . . . wherefore I thynke yow maye doo good yff yow can have money." This seems to refer, not to the loan Richard had asked for, but to a proposed bargain with Shakespeare.[21]

Richard Quiney the younger, a schoolboy of eleven, wrote a letter in Latin asking his father to buy copybooks ("*chartaceos libellos*") for him and his brother. His mother Bess, who could not write herself, reminded her husband through Sturley to buy the apron he had promised her and "a suite of hattes for 5 boies the yongst lined & trimmed with silke" (for John, only a year old). A letter signed "Isabell Bardall" entreated "Good Cozen" Quiney to find her stepson Adrian, son of George Bardell, a place in London with some handicraftsman. William Parsons and William Walford, drapers, asked Quiney to see to business matters in London. Daniel Baker deluged his "Unckle Quyne" with requests to pay money for him to drapers in Watling Street and at the Two Cats in Canning Street. His letter of October 26 named two of the men about whom Quiney had written to Shakespeare the day before. Baker wrote: "I tooke order with Sr E. Grevile for the payment of Ceartaine monie beefore his going towardes London. & synce I did write unto him to dessier him to paie 10^{li} for mee which standeth mee greatly uppon to have paide. & xx[11] more m[r] peeter Rowswell tooke order with his master to paie for mee." He asked Quiney to find out whether the money had been paid and, if not, to send to the lodging of Sir Edward and entreat him to pay what he owed. Baker added: "I pray you delivre these inclosed Letters And Comend mee to m[r] Rychard mytton whoe I know will ffreind mee for the payment of this monie." Further letters in November mention that Sir Edward paid forty pounds.[22]

Stratford's petition to the queen declared that two great fires had burnt two hundred houses in the town, with household goods, to the value of twelve thousand pounds. The chancellor of the Exchequer wrote on the petition: "in myn opinion it is very resonable and conscionable for hir ma*ie*stie to graunt in relief of this towne twise afflicted and almost wasted by fire." The queen agreed on December 17, a warrant was signed on January 27, and the Exchequer paid Quiney his expenses on February 27, 1598/9. He listed what he had spent for "My own diet in London eighteen weeks, in which I was sick a month; my mare at coming up 14 days; another I bought there to bring me home 7 weeks; and I was six days going thither and coming homewards; all which cost me at the least £20." He was allowed forty-four pounds in all, including fees to the masters of requests, Mr. Fanshawe of the Exchequer, the solicitor general, and other oficials and their clerks. If he borrowed money from Shakespeare or with his help, he would now have been able to repay the loan.[23]

Since more is known about Quiney than about any other acquaintance of Shakespeare in Stratford, his career may be followed to its sudden end in 1602. During 1598 and 1599 he made "manye Guiftes of myne owne provision bestowed uppon Cowrtiers & others for the better effectinge of our suites in hande." He was in London "searching records for our town's causes" in 1600 with young Henry Sturley, the assistant schoolmaster. When Sir Edward Greville enclosed the town commons on the Bancroft, Quiney and others leveled his hedges on January 21, 1600/1, and were charged with riot by Sir Edward. He also sued them for taking toll of grain at their market. Accompanied by "Master Greene our solicitor" (Thomas Greene of the Middle Temple, Shakespeare's "cousin"), Quiney tried to consult Sir Edward Coke, attorney general, and gave money to a clerk and a doorkeeper "that we might have access to their master for his counsel . . . butt colde nott have him att Leasure by the reason of thees trobles" (the Essex rising on February 8). He set down that "I gave m^r Greene a pynte of muskadell and a roll of bread that last morning I went to have his company to Master Attorney." After returning to Stratford he drew up a defense of the town's right to toll corn and the office of collecting it, and his list of suggested witnesses included his father and Shakespeare's father. No one, he wrote, took any corn of Greville's, for his bailiff of husbandry "swore a greate oathe thatt whoe soe came to put hys hande into hys sackes for anye corne shuld leave hys hande be hynde hym." Quiney was in London again in June, 1601, and in November, when he rode up, as Shakespeare must often have done, by way of Oxford, High Wycombe, and Uxbridge, and home through Aylesbury and Banbury.[24]

After Quiney was elected bailiff in September, 1601, without Greville's approval, Greene wrote him that Coke had promised to be of counsel for Stratford and had advised "that the office of bayly may be exercised as it is taken upon you, (Sr Edwardes his consent not beinge hadd to the swearinge of you)." Asked by the townsmen to cease his suit, Greville had answered that "hytt shulde coste hym 500^{11} first & sayed it must be tried ether before my Lorde Anderson in the countrey or his uncle ffortescue in the exchequer with whom he colde more prevaile then we." The corporation proposed Chief Justice Anderson for an arbiter, sending him a gift of sack and claret. Lady Greville, daughter of the late Lord Chancellor Bromley and niece of Sir John Fortescue, was offered twenty pounds by the townsmen to make peace; she "labored & thought she shuld effecte" it but her husband said that "we shuld wynne it by the sworde." His servant Robin Whitney threatened Quiney, who had Whitney bound to "the good abaringe" to keep the peace. A report of "Sr Edw: Grevyles minaces to the Baileefe Aldermen & Burgesses of Stratforde" tells how Quiney was injured by Greville's men: "in the tyme m^r Ryc' Quyney was bayleefe ther came some of them whoe beinge druncke fell to braweling in ther hosts howse wher thei druncke & drewe ther dagers uppon the hoste: att a faier tyme the Baileefe being late abroade to see the towne in order & comminge by in y^t hurley Burley. came into the howse & commawnded the peace to be kept butt colde nott prevayle & in hys endevor to sticle the brawle had his heade grevouselye brooken by one of hys [Greville's] men whom nether hym selfe [Greville] punnished nor wolde suffer to be punnished but with a shewe to turne them awaye & enterteyned agayne." On May 3, 1602, Quiney kept the tollbook of horses sold or exchanged at Stratford fair. He was wounded that night or the next and did not outlive the month, for the register notes the burial on May 31 of "Mr. Richard Quiny, Bailey of Stretforde."[25]

Quiney, who died without making a will, left his widow Elizabeth with nine children, all under twenty: Elizabeth, Adrian, Richard, Thomas, Anne, William, Mary, John, and George. Richard (1587–1656) became a grocer at the Red Lion in Bucklersbury, London, and with his partner John Sadler gave Stratford a mace and bought two plantations in Virginia, Martin's Brandon and Merchant's Hope. Thomas, born in 1589, was a vintner and married Judith Shakespeare. George (1600–1624) took his degree at Balliol and served as curate and usher at Stratford till he died of consumption. John Hall described him as "of a good wit and expert in languages."[26]

The only townsman known to have attended a university before 1595, other than schoolmasters and clergy, was Abraham Sturley or Strelly, a student in 1569 at Queens' College, Cambridge. One of his letters to Quiney is all in Latin, others partly in Latin, and he advised his friend, "Read Tully's Epistles." He took great care in 1607 to price each of a hundred and seventy books left by a clergyman, John Marshall, including two copies of Cicero's epistles in Latin. Sturley held some office under Sir Thomas Lucy in 1573 and 1580. He married in 1575 Anne, daughter of Richard

Hill, then bailiff, and after living for a few years at Worcester settled in Stratford. Though he twice declined to serve on the town council, he accepted in 1591 and was alderman and chamberlain by 1594. The records he kept are unusually full, and the town petitioned the queen that he might be sworn a public notary. While he was bailiff in 1596–97 he rewarded four companies of players and a show of the city of Norwich. He bestowed "a drinking of peares & wine" on Mr. Robert Burgoyne and Sir John Conway, and a pottle of claret on Mr. Barton. Plague struck in the same year, and he lost his son Thomas and his servant Thomas Edkins, possibly related to Shakespeare's uncle of the same name. His son Richard entered Balliol in 1597 and his eldest son Henry came from Oxford to teach at Stratford school until 1604, after which he was vicar at Chipping Campden and Broadway. "Mr Sturly and Richard Queene and Mr Badger" were described in 1595 as "great Corne byeres and byeres of woode and such lycke." Sturley had twenty-four persons in his household and Quiney sixteen. In 1598 Sturley had malt belonging to Sir Thomas Lucy, Mr. Anthony Nash, and Mr. Richard Willis. In this year he rode to Cambridge and Bedford to gather money for sufferers from the fires in Stratford. His house in Wood Street had burnt in 1594, but in his valuable survey of town property in 1599 he reported that he had "sett up of newe xij. baies" and must finish covering all sixteen bays with tile instead of thatch. Meanwhile he was living in 1597 in another house in "Winsore" near Henley Street. He sent news from Stratford to his "dear brother in the Lord" Quiney, sometimes writing for Mrs. Quiney his "sister" by candlelight "att ur owne table in ur owne house," or describing Quiney's father as "extraordinari hartie, chearefull, and lustie." With Quiney he rode to see Lord Burghley in 1593 and to consult Bishop Babington at Worcester in 1601. His most successful mission was in 1610, when he and Daniel Baker secured a new charter for Stratford. He was buried in 1614 as Mr. Abraham Sturley, gentleman.[27]

Adrian Quiney had told Sturley in 1598 that Shakespeare was willing to buy land in Shottery or elsewhere near Stratford. On

May 1, 1602, William Shakespere of Stratford upon Avon, gentleman, bought land in Old Stratford from William Combe of Warwick, esquire, and John Combe of Old Stratford, gentleman. The deed was "Sealed and delivered to Gilbert Shakespere to the use of the within named William Shakespere in the presence of Anthony Nasshe, William Sheldon, Humfrey Maynwaringe, Rychard Mason, Jhon Nashe." For three hundred and twenty pounds paid in full Shakespeare acquired in fee simple "fowre yarde lande of errable lande . . . Conteyninge by estimacion One hundred and Seaven acres be they more or lesse And also all the Common pasture for Sheepe horse kyne or other Cattle in the feildes of Olde Stretford aforesaide to the said ffowre yarde lande belonginge or in any wise apperteyninge And also all hades leys tyinges proffittes advantages and Commodities whatsoever . . . hertofore reputed taken knowne or occupied as parte parcell or member of the same." The land was "nowe or late in the severall tenures or occupacions of Thomas Hiccoxe and Lewes Hiccoxe." The Combes promised to make further assurance in law if required within five years, and a fine was accordingly entered in the court of Common Pleas, though not until 1610. Since the fine or final concord was a fictitious action at law to confirm the title, the one hundred pounds which Shakespeare is said to have paid for this acknowledgment was probably also fictitious. The fine described Shakespeare's purchase as one hundred and seven acres of land and twenty acres of pasture, the same amount bought in 1593 by William Combe. The pasture, therefore, was part of the land he sold in 1602. The deed to Shakespeare conveyed land "within the parrishe feildes or towne of Olde Stretford," but Shakespeare's will devised property in Old Stratford, Bishopton, and Welcombe. Though most records describe it as in Old Stratford, this land was regarded as part of Bishopton in 1634, when John Hall as Shakespeare's heir owned four yardlands out of seventeen and a half in "the whole town" of Bishopton.[28]

William Clopton had sold in 1570 to Rice Griffin estates which included this land and Ingon Meadow, held by John Shakespeare.

William Combe bought in 1593 from Rice Griffin the land which he and his nephew John sold to Shakespeare. He owned other land in Old Stratford, for which he was on the subsidy roll in 1605–6 and 1609–10. William Combe, the posthumous son of John Combe of Stratford, who died in 1550, was born at Broadway in June, 1551, and was buried at St. Nicholas, Warwick, on October 5, 1610. On *A Profitable Book of the Laws of England* (now at Stratford) he wrote "Cest le liver de Gulihelme Combes" and the date of his admission to the Middle Temple in 1571. In religion he was Anglican, not Puritan, for he was trusted by Whitgift and served as an ecclesiastical commissioner from 1601 to 1608. A member of parliament for Droitwich in 1588, for the town of Warwick in 1593, and for the county in 1597, he was chosen reader at the Middle Temple in 1595 and counsel for Stratford in 1597. The corporation sent wine to him and Lady Puckering when they were at the College in 1606, and when he became sheriff the next year they gave him a keg of sturgeon for a New Year's gift. Queen Elizabeth had granted him in 1594 leases of the Vineyard House and the Castle mills at Warwick, but after he married his second wife Jane, widow of Sir John Puckering, lord keeper, he lived at the Priory in Warwick. Here he made his will on April 1, 1610, naming as heirs his nephew John and his great-nephew William of Stratford, with generous bequests to the poor of Warwick and Stratford and of Broadway and Alvechurch in Worcestershire. His nephew John Combe of Stratford left a bequest of five pounds in 1613 "to Mr William Shackspere."[29]

Shakespeare's tenants were Thomas and Lewis Hiccox, but there were several men of these names. A "Thomas Hiccocks junior" had been admitted tenant at Welcombe in 1552. Thomas Hiccox of Welcombe, husbandman, died in 1606, leaving goods valued at eighty pounds by Peter Roswell, Abraham Sturley, and John Smith. His will named his wife Alice (d. 1607) and six children: Richard, William, Thomas, Lewis (who was christened at Stratford on February 12, 1564/5), Anne or Annes Barton, and Isabel. His son Thomas, born in 1562, may have been the "Thomas

Hiccockes junior" who bought property from Richard Quiney in 1591, the Thomas who in 1600 married Elizabeth, daughter of Abraham Sturley, and the Thomas who leased a house in Henley Street in 1599 and died in 1611. The grain returns of 1595 mention that Thomas of Welcombe "usethe husbandrye" and must send barley and malt to Stratford market weekly. They also mention, under "Wood Street and Back Street," Stratford, that Lewis Hiccox "usethe husbandrye" but that his wife brewed and sold ale without license. Though he was living in Bridge Street ward in 1598, by 1603 Lewis was a licensed innholder in Henley Street, where his wife Alice quarreled in that year with a neighbor's wife at the Bell Inn. Probably he leased the eastern house which had belonged to John Shakespeare and which in 1642 was called the Maidenhead Inn. His wife Alice, "old goody hicox," testified in 1616 that a tinker's wife "came up ye gilpits & in at the backyate" of her house. Although another Thomas Hiccox worked for the Combes, Lewis Hiccox "disagreed to the intended inclosure" at Welcombe, where he held land from Mrs. Reynolds. He and Laurence Wheeler were the tenants in 1618 of Mr. Hall's land, formerly Shakespeare's. Wheeler, who lived in Henley Street, had married the widow of Lewis's brother Thomas. When Lewis Hiccox died in 1627 he was succeeded by a Thomas Hiccox, whose widow Jane later occupied the Henley Street inn as tenant to Susanna Hall. Lewis Hiccox, then, kept an inn in Henley Street next to the Birthplace and also farmed Shakespeare's land at Bishopton.[30]

Since Shakespeare owned land at Bishopton, he probably knew the minister of the chapel there, John Marshall, an Oxford B.A. in 1575 and M.A. in 1577. "John Marshall, minister," was curate in 1599 both of Bishopton and of Bearley, where he signed the register in 1601 with his churchwarden John Hill, son of Agnes Arden. In his will, made at Bishopton on January 30, 1606/7, he mentioned bonds owing from his father-in-law Ralph Lorde of Stratford and from Stephen Burman the elder and the younger of Shottery, and left "all my bookes which are not more specially bestowed" to be divided among his three sons at the age of fourteen "accordinge to everie ons fitnes to use the same." Sturley wrote the will and a careful inventory, the only full list of a Stratford library in Shakespeare's time. He named and priced one hundred and seventy books, mainly religious works or schoolbooks, with a Greek Testament and Greek and Hebrew grammars. The English books include a work on versification now lost, "Beverley, *English Meeter*"; *The Art of Angling* (1577), long unknown but rediscovered in 1954; Ascham's *Schoolmaster;* Elyot's *Castle of Health;* Gifford's *Discourse of Witchcraft;* More's *Apology; Pasquin's Trance; The Voyage of the Wandering Knight;* and *Terra Florida,* described as a pamphlet and probably the book of 1563 by Jean Ribaut, *The Whole and True Discovery of Terra Florida, (Englished the Florishing Lande).* Halliwell-Phillipps found lining a box of town records at Stratford several sheets of Captain Best's book of 1578 describing Frobisher's "voyages of discoverie for the finding of a passage to Cathaya by the Northweast."[31]

After buying land for three hundred and twenty pounds, Shakespeare in 1605 invested four hundred and forty pounds in the purchase of a lease of tithes at Stratford. He acquired from Ralph Hubaud of Ipsley, esquire, on July 24, 1605, a half-share in the "tythes of corne, grayne, blade, and heye" from Old Stratford, Welcombe, and Bishopton and in the "tythes of wooll, lambe, and other smalle and pryvie tythes" from the parish of Stratford, except for certain tithes of Luddington and Bishopton and certain rights of Lord Carew and Sir Edward Greville. Shakespeare paid yearly rents of five pounds to John Barker and seventeen pounds to the bailiff and burgesses of Stratford, who were to receive these tithes when the lease expired in 1636. He entrusted the management of his tithes to his friend Anthony Nash of Welcombe, who was paying the rent to the town in 1606 with Thomas Combe and in 1614 with William Combe. The tithes brought Shakespeare sixty pounds a year, according to a Chancery bill, and this was over and above the rents, as Thomas Greene made clear in 1617 when he valued his half-share of the same tithes at £71 13s. 4d., all rents deducted. Greene's estimate was high, since he finally sold his lease for four hundred pounds instead of the price he asked, five hundred and fifty pounds for the tithes of grain and forty pounds for the small tithes. Shakespeare's heirs, John and Susanna Hall, on March 1, 1624/5 sold all but a small part of their half to the corporation, also for four hundred pounds, and the yearly value of their share was then ninety pounds, less twenty-two pounds in rents, leaving an income of sixty-eight pounds.[32]

The name "Hubaud" has usually been misread as "Huband," though Stratford records spelled it "Hubalt," "Hubatt," "Hewbottes," "Hybote," or "Hawbutt." Ralph Hubaud sold to Shakespeare the tithe-rights bequeathed to him in 1583 by his brother Sir John Hubaud, constable of Kenilworth Castle under Leicester and a knight of the shire in parliament. Sir John also left a grant of silver mines to his brother and to George Digby. Ralph married at Broadway in 1584 Anne, daughter of Anthony Daston and his wife Anne Sheldon of Beoley. In the year of the Armada he came to Stratford to muster the trained men and in 1592 he was sheriff of Warwickshire. His tithes were farmed in 1596 by Thomas Combe and Richard Quiney. As a justice he supported Stratford's petition for relief in 1598. When he died, soon after selling the tithes, the inventory of the estate of the right worshipful Mr. Ralph Hubaud, made on January 31, 1605/6, listed a debt of twenty pounds "Owinge by Mr. Shakespre." He owed money to his brother-in-law Mr. Walter Savage, and Walter Savage Landor later inherited his manor of Ipsley.[33]

Shakespeare received a good income from his tithes, and to protect his rights he joined in a plea of equity to Lord Chancellor Ellesmere. Richard Lane of Alveston, esquire, Thomas Greene of Stratford, esquire, and William Shakespeare of Stratford, gentleman, brought a Chancery suit in 1610 or 1610/11 against George Lord Carew of Clopton, Sir Edward Greville, Sir Edward Conway, Mary and William Combe, and Henry Barker. Barker was assign of his father, John Barker, whose monument at Hurst in Berkshire records that he had been for thirty-four years gentleman usher to Queen Elizabeth and that he died in 1620. John Barker, esquire, came to Stratford in 1612 to testify about tithes. The town had tried to buy the Barker lease in May, 1610, offering ten times the yearly rent, but Henry Barker was now threatening to repossess the tithes and other property which his father in 1580 had sub-leased to Sir John Hubaud, unless he received his full yearly rent of £27 13s. 4d. within forty days after Michaelmas and Lady Day when he demanded payment "at the porch of the parishe Church of Stratford." Shakespeare paid five pounds of this rent and five pounds were due from the holder of the other half of the same tithes, William Combe of Stratford. Shakespeare and his fellow-plaintiffs explained that the rest of the rent was due from forty others who had derived estates from Sir John Hubaud, and these "could never yet be drawn to agree howe to paye the residue of the said rente," so that "Richard Lane and William Shackspeare, and some fewe others of the said parties, are wholly, and against all equity and good conscience, usually dryven to pay the same." Others "have given yt forth that they should be glade and Cared not a Whitt yf the estates of some or all the said premisses should be forfeyted for they should doe well enoughe with the sayd Henry Barker." The plaintiffs asked for a Chancery commission to examine witnesses and assess payments towards the rent. William Combe answered on February 13, 1610/11, that he was paying his five pounds and was willing to pay his share for other tithes. After Combe's lease ended, Thomas Greene in 1617 sold to the corporation his lease of half the tithes of grain in Old Stratford, Welcombe, and Bishopton, valuing his share as bringing in a hundred marks a year more than the rents, and of half the offerings and small tithes in Stratford, valuing his share as worth five pounds a year. He noted that "There are faire Barnes for the layinge in of these tythes of Corne & graine," near the College House. The fields he listed were those from which Shakespeare also had gathered half the tithes of wool and lamb: thirty-two yardlands in the common fields of Old Stratford with "50 sheepe every yard land," seventeen in Bishopton, forty-two and a half in Shottery, and other land in Drayton, Clopton, Bridgetown, Ryne Clifford, and Bushwood. Shakespeare's rights included half the small tithes of calves, kids, pigs, geese, poultry, and eggs, of woods and coppices, of Stratford mills, and of the fishing in the Avon.[34]

Shakespeare sued in the Stratford court of record in 1608 to recover a debt of six pounds from John Addenbrooke, gentleman. The case proceeded from August 17, 1608, to June 7, 1609. Addenbrooke was arrested but freed when he produced a surety, Thomas Hornby, and a jury in 1608/9 awarded Shakespeare his debt with costs and damages. Since Addenbrooke could not be found in Stratford, Shakespeare sought his money from Hornby, a blacksmith who kept an alehouse in Henley Street. Hornby was often a surety, and the corporation sued him in 1613 as surety for Hamlet Smith's bequest. The debtor was not a Stratford man, but a John Addenbrooke bought the advowson of Tanworth in 1584 and sold it the next year, and in 1594 recovered a debt of forty shillings from John Armstrong at Stratford. About 1600 an Addenbrooke was selling licenses to make starch in Warwickshire. Another suitor in the court of record in 1608 was Florisell Bovey of Alcester, whose name recalls the hero of one of the Amadis romances and Shakespeare's prince in *The Winter's Tale*.[35]

Curiously little is on record about Shakespeare's brothers, Gilbert, Richard, and Edmund. Richard's life is a blank between his baptism on March 11, 1573/4, and his burial on February 4, 1612/13. Edmund, baptized on May 3, 1580, became an actor in London. "Edward sonne of Edward Shackspeere, Player: baseborne" was buried at St. Giles, Cripplegate, on August 12, 1607, and "Edmond Shakespeare a player in the Church" at St. Saviour's, Southwark, on December 31, 1607. A fee of twenty shillings was paid at St. Saviour's, probably by Shakespeare, to have Edmund "buried in the Church with a forenoone knell of the great bell." This was the winter of the great frost, when the Thames froze above London Bridge before Christmas.[36]

Gilbert Shakespeare, baptized on October 3, 1566, lived both in

Stratford and in London. In Trinity term, 1597, "Gilbert Shack-spere" of St. Bride's, haberdasher, gave surety in Queen's Bench, with Richard Johnson of St. Bride's, shoemaker, for William Sampson of Stratford on Avon, "Clookmaker" (clockmaker, for the parish of St. Nicholas in Warwick sent their clock to Stratford to be mended by "Sampson the Clocksmithe"). On May 1, 1602, he acted for his brother William in taking delivery of the deed to land in Old Stratford, probably with the usual livery of seisin by turf and twig. He signed his name "Gilbart Shakesper" in a neat Italian hand as witness on March 5, 1609/10, to a lease of property in Bridge Street, Stratford, made by Margery, widow of Ralph Lorde, to her son Richard Smith alias Court. The Stratford register records the burial on February 3, 1611/12, of "Gilbert Shak-speare, adolescens." The last word seems here to mean "single," for the register often used "adolocentulus" and "adolocentula" to describe persons who were adult but unmarried.[37]

I have found one new reference to Gilbert Shakespeare, and I hope that others will be found when certain records of the court of Requests for the reign of James I, now withdrawn for calendar-ing, are again open to search. Sir Christopher Parkins, one of the masters of requests, issued this order on November 21, 1609: "ffiat breve de P. S. directum Ricardo Mytton Petro vswell [read Ruswell] Roberto Wilson Georgio Heigham mariae Burnell et Gilberto Shackespeare Ad Comparendum Imediate Ad respond-endum Johannae Bromley et hoc sub pena C[11]." The writ of privy seal or subpena directing "Peter Ruswell and others" to answer in Hilary term became the subject of affidavits by Thomas Lucas of Gray's Inn, William Osborn of Stratford, yeoman, and Elionor Varney, servant to Joan Bromley of Stratford, widow. Elionor, a girl of twenty-one, declared that when she served "Ruswell" with the writ, he "did vyolently snatche from her the said writt and refused to redeliver it unto her, and delivered his staffe he then had in his hand to a stander by who therewith did assault & beate this deponent out of the house." Widow Bromley's bill of complaint, may or may not be preserved at the Record Office. If it could be found, it would explain the reason for the suit.[38]

The Stratford register shows that Edward Bromley married Joan Bell in 1579 and died in 1606 and that one Joan Bromley, widow, died in 1621 and another in 1625. Bromley was a recusant in 1592, and Sturley wrote to Quiney in 1598 "a long letter for our long carrier, Edward Bromley, to have brought you." He had a license to sell ale and left an estate worth eighty-three pounds. His widow Joan sued on a bill for carriage of a barrel of figs from London.[39]

The most interesting co-defendants with Gilbert Shakespeare were the "m^r Mytton" and "m^r Rosswell" of Quiney's letter to Shakespeare. Richard Mytton, an officer of Sir Edward Greville, was grandson of Richard Mytton of Shrewsbury, who had married the daughter of an earlier Sir Edward Greville. A letter from a fellow-attendant at Milcote prays "good m^r Mitton" to buy him Milan fustian in London and hopes that God will "send my Ladye her helth and my master good newes of his shipe." Daniel Baker mentioned both Mr. Mytton and Mr. "Rowswell." Ralph Hubaud and others in 1605 acknowledged a fine conveying property in Ipsley to Richard Mytton, gentleman, and others. Mytton was sued in 1608 for saying to Sir John Harrington of Elmesthorpe, Leicestershire, "Hackett is a Theefe and hathe stollen your haye and Carried itt awaye by nighte."[40]

John Smith, vintner, wrote in his will in 1601, "I desire the righte worshipfull Sr Edward Greevill, my brother Francis Smithe, and my lovinge freind Peter Ruswell to be Overseers." Roswell joined with his master's brother Peter Greville to obtain a crown grant, which they assigned to Sir Edward in 1601, of property that had once belonged to Stratford College. Peter Roswell of Welcombe, gentleman, owned freehold near Shakespeare's and told Sir Henry Rainsford in 1615 that he would sue William Combe for trespass in carrying away his corn, and in Star Chamber for riots, and that Sir Edward Greville "would stick to him." He witnessed the wills of Thomas and Alice Hiccox and appraised their estates, and Peter and John Roswell witnessed the deed by which Bartholomew Hathaway bought Hewlands in 1610. The register has several signatures of Peter Roswell as a churchwarden from 1608 to 1610, and it records the burial in 1630 of his wife Elizabeth and on December 6, 1633, of "Mr Peter Ruswell."[41]

According to Aubrey, Shakespeare "was wont to goe to his native Country once a yeare." Most of his visits are likely to have been during the summer. When Hubaud signed the indenture for tithes on July 24, 1605, Shakespeare must have signed the counterpart, which has not survived. Presumably he attended the wedding of his daughter Susanna to John Hall on June 5, 1607. Through an attorney he began suit against John Addenbrooke at Stratford in August, 1608, and on October 16 he was godfather to William Walker, either in person or by proxy. Though there is no direct evidence, he may have been at Stratford for the funerals of his son in August, 1596, of his father in September, 1601, and of his mother in September, 1608. But even in his last years there are few dates on which he is known for certain to have been in Stratford.

CHAPTER VIII

SHAKESPEARE'S

FRIENDS

❖Shakespeare in his will named several of his friends in or near Stratford, placing special trust in John Hall, Thomas Russell, and Francis Collins. Among his friends in the town who were no longer alive in 1616 the only one now traceable is John Combe, who left a bequest to Shakespeare. Thomas Greene, though not mentioned in the will, had lived in Shakespeare's house and set down in his diary what Shakespeare said to him and to his brother John. This chapter will bring together what is known about the friends who are named in the will, about the Combe family, and about Thomas and John Greene.

John Hall married Susanna Shakespeare on June 5, 1607, and lived at New Place from 1616 or earlier until his death on November 25, 1635, aged sixty. He was thus about eleven years younger than Shakespeare. Born in Bedfordshire, he matriculated at Cambridge in 1589 from Queens' College, proceeding B.A. in 1593/4 and M.A. in 1597. Although he studied medicine, he never took a doctor's degree. The editor of his *Select Observations* wrote that "He had been a Traveller acquainted with the *French* tongue," but the only evidence for this seems to be that Hall quoted in French a medical work by Jean Liébault. His father was also a physician, William Hall of Acton, Middlesex, gentleman, whose will was made on December 12, 1607, and proved by John on December 24 at London. William Hall left to John "all my bookes of phisicke," "unto my man Mathewe Morris all my bookes of Astronomye and Astrologie" on condition that he give instruction "yf my sonne John do intende and purpose to laboure studdye and endevor in the sayed Arte," and to Morris "all my bookes of Alchimye." Morris followed John to Stratford, married there in 1613, named children Susanna and John, and acted as a trustee for Susanna Hall in 1617/18. John Hall's father may have been "William, my brother Robert Hall's son," named in 1557 in the will of William Hall, gentleman, of Bedford, apparently a former mayor of that town. William Hall of Acton lived at Carlton in Bedfordshire from 1569 to 1593, and eleven of his children are mentioned either in the Carlton register or in his will or in both: Elizabeth, Susan, Sara (who married William Shepherd, M.D., fellow of King's College, Cambridge, and a physician at Leicester), Samuel, Dive (not recorded at Carlton but named for a Bedfordshire family), John (not recorded at Carlton but, like his brother Dive, described at Cambridge as born in Bedfordshire), Frances (not recorded at Carlton but married to Michael Welles, who was born there in 1578, the son of the rector), Martha, Mary, Damaris, and William. Dive Hall, whose father's will mentioned "the many unkyndnes which he showed unto me heretofore and especially synce the deathe of his mother," died at Acton in 1626, leaving whatever remained of his portion to his brother-in-law Michael Welles. Three years later Welles, then of Glatton, Hunts, brought a Chancery suit against John Hall of Stratford, who answered that he had agreed to give up the executorship of his father's will "in regard it would be a hinderance to the defendant in his profession being a Phisitian." Shakespeare's granddaughter Elizabeth left a bequest to her cousin Thomas Welles of Carlton (1603–1670).[1]

"Elizabeth dawghter to John Hall gentleman" was christened on February 21, 1607/8. New Place is the only house in which the Halls are known to have lived, though the name Hall's Croft has been given to an attractive house in Old Town near the church, now owned by the Birthplace Trust. Hall bought from Abraham

Sturley in 1612 "a close by Evesham way," but there is no proof that he ever lived outside the borough.[2]

Mrs. Susanna Hall brought suit for defamation in the consistory court at Worcester Cathedral on July 15, 1613, against John Lane the younger, because "about 5. weekes past the def*endan*t reported that the pl*aintiff* had the runinge of the raynes & had bin naught with Rafe Smith at John Palmer." Robert Whatcott appeared for Mrs. Hall, but Lane did not appear and was excommunicated on July 27. Ralph Smith, haberdasher and hatter, was born in 1577, the son of John Smith, vintner, and nephew of Hamnet Sadler, who gave surety for him in 1599. He married before 1605 and in that year conveyed property to William Smith. As a soldier in the trained band he had his gun repaired at the time of the Gunpowder Plot, and "A bible of Ralph Smythes" was in the inventory of John Marshall. Often foreman of the jury at sessions, he sued George Jennings for assault in 1612. He was mentioned again with Lane in 1619 and in 1621, the year of his death. John Lane the younger (1590–1640) was sued in Star Chamber in 1619 for riot and libels against the vicar and aldermen and was presented by the church-wardens as a drunkard. His brother Nicholas was summoned in 1607 "for a ffraye and blud shed on m^r Tho Lucas." Their uncle Richard Lane, esquire, made John Hall a trustee for his children on July 9, 1613.[3]

Hall was at London in 1614, with Shakespeare, and again in 1616 to prove Shakespeare's will. He refused to be made a knight by Charles I, preferring to pay a fine of ten pounds. Though he gave the church a carved pulpit and was churchwarden in 1628–29, he declined to serve on the town council until 1632, when the council for the third time elected "Jo Hall generosus, in Artibus Magister." Too busy as a physician to attend meetings, he argued with the bailiff and aldermen and was dismissed in 1633. He joined his friend the vicar, Thomas Wilson, in a Chancery suit against the corporation, declaring that he had sold the tithes for a hundred pounds less than their worth so that the town might increase the vicar's salary. By an oral will on November 25, 1635, Hall left

his goods and money to his wife and daughter, his house in Acton
to his daughter, and to her husband Thomas Nash his "Study of
Bookes" and his manuscripts. The manuscripts would have been
given, if he had been present, to "Mr. Boles," Joseph Bowles of
Chapel Street, M.A. at Cambridge in 1634 from Emmanuel College. Mrs. Hall and Nash declared in Chancery that Hall's goods
were worth at least a thousand pounds and that "Divers bookes"
and other valuables had been seized by bailiffs in 1636 to satisfy
a debt. Two manuscripts written by Hall, "both intended for the
press," were bought from Mrs. Hall during the Civil War by Lord
Brooke's surgeon, James Cooke of Warwick, who translated parts
from Latin and published in 1657 Hall's *Select Observations on
English Bodies*. One of these manuscripts is at the British Museum,
Egerton MS 2065.[4]

Hall described "no lesse than a thousand" observations of his
cures, one hundred and seventy-eight of which were printed, the
earliest dated case from 1617. He cured his daughter Elizabeth
with a fomentation of aqua vitae and spices. "Browne a Romish
Priest labouring of an Ungarick [Hungarian or typhus] Fever in
danger of death" was saved with the help of a powder of leaf
gold, pearls, and "fragments of jacynt, Smerdines and Rubyes."
Sir Thomas Puckering of Warwick, baronet and M.P., who had
been educated with Prince Henry, Hall described as very learned,
much given to study, of lean constitution yet phlegmatic; and he
cured the Stratford schoolmaster, John Trapp, who "by much study
fell into hypochondriack melancholy." He used rhubarb and
"Seny," the purgative drugs mentioned by Macbeth, to purge Captain Basset's melancholy. The Earl and Countess of Northampton
often sent for Hall to come to Ludlow Castle when the earl was
president of Wales, and he cured the second earl of a pleurisy got
"by following his Hounds in a cold and rainy day." One of his
patients was restored to health in London by the famous Dr. William Harvey, whose prescription is given. Hall treated Bishop
Thornborough of Worcester, a companion of Lyly at Oxford and
now over eighty, who "was long tormented with a scorbutick

wandering gout" and had terror in his sleep because of a sudden
slaughter in his household which afflicted him with melancholy.
Hall had cured his own wife of scurvy, and he gave the bishop
his special "Scorbutick beer," five gallons boiled with scurvy grass,
water cress, fumitory, fennel, and juniper berries. He attended Sir
Thomas Temple, who had desired vine sets from New Place, for
Lady Tyrrell wrote to Lady Temple at Wolverton, Bucks, "I am
very glad to hear: that M^r halle: Is the mann: of hom: Sr Thomas
Tempell: hath made choice of: In regard I kno by experyence:
that hee is most excelent In that arte." Sir Edward Tyrrell added to
his wife's letter, "I am sorie to heare of Sr Thomas Temples mis-
fortun. gett mr hale speedilie to him." Sidney Davenport wrote in
1632 insisting that Hall attend him instead of a council meeting,
arguing that for a physician to be a member of a corporation would
"indaunger the liefe of his patient for want of his presence" and
that the magistrates ought not "to lay this burthen uppon you
whose profession is to be most abroad." Hall survived a dangerous
fever "About the 57 year of my age, August. 27. 1632," but
"Johannes Hall, medicus peritissimus," was buried near Shakespeare in 1635 and "good Mistris Hall," "Witty above her sexe,"
in 1649.[5]

Hall's most interesting record is of "Mr Drayton poeta laure-
atus," whom he cured of a tertian fever by an emetic infusion
mixed with syrup of violets. Drayton was probably visiting the
Rainsfords at Clifford Chambers, Gloucestershire, within two miles
of Stratford. He paid tribute in *Poly-Olbion* (1612) to

> deere *Cliffords* seat (the place of health and sport)
> Which many a time hath been the Muses quiet Port.

In the last year of his life, 1631, he wrote to Drummond from
Clifford, "a Knight's House in *Glocester-Shire,* to which Place I
Yearly use to come, in the Summer Time, to recreate my self, and
to spend some Two or Three Months in the Country." Hall treated
several Rainsfords, including Drayton's Idea, Anne Goodere, born
about 1571 and married to Henry Rainsford in 1595. He described

her as Lady Rainsford, about sixty-two, modest, pious, kindly, de-
voted to the reading of sacred literature, and expert in French and
Italian. Drayton wrote an elegy on the death in 1621/2 of "his
incomparable friend" Sir Henry Rainsford. Sir Henry took an interest in Stratford affairs, for he wrote in 1607 asking the bailiff,
Shakespeare's friend Henry Walker, to appoint William Daulkes
as a sergeant at mace after the death of Edward Ange, who "is
rather for heaven then to Intertayne any hope of this world." He
was a witness and overseer of the will of Thomas Combe, his son
Henry's godfather, and an overseer of the will of John Combe,
who gave a ring to Lady Rainsford and five pounds each to Sir
Henry and to Shakespeare. The town council asked Sir Henry in
1614/15 to write his opinion to Mr. Mainwaring, "whoe as S^r
Henry Raynsford hath affirmed to m^r Baker as m^r Baker here
affirmeth will thereuppon surceass from further inclosure." He told
Greene of his conversations with William Combe, John Nash, and
Peter Roswell. When the town was collecting for sufferers from
fire, he gave generously and asked the lord chancellor to renew the
patent. A patent of his own in 1616 licensed him to make a park
and free warren at Clifford or Alveston. Next year he arranged
terms between Greene and the council, giving his word that Greene
would perform the agreement, and Greene wrote of "the respect I
beare to that worthy Knight." The council gave Mrs. Greene five
pounds "for her Love in the name of a gratuetie, At S^r the Right
woorshipfulle Sr Henry Rainsford his Request."[6]

Shakespeare left five pounds to Thomas Russell, esquire, and
entreated Russell to be an overseer of his will. Malone found the
will of Russell, but Dr. Hotson first clearly identified this friend of
Shakespeare and discovered all that is known of his life. Russell
was born in 1570, the son of Sir Thomas of Strensham, Worcestershire, a Protestant member of parliament and trusted adviser to
Bishop Sandys. Sir Thomas died in 1574 and left Thomas leases of
two manors, Broad Campden and Alderminster. Brought up at
Bruton, Somerset, by his mother and her second husband, Sir
Henry Berkeley, Thomas entered Queen's College, Oxford, in

1588. Two years later he married Katherine, daughter of Hugh Bampfield, esquire, but death took her and their two daughters, Margaret and Jane. He was Thomas Russell of Bruton, esquire, in a bond of 1591, joined with his friend Henry Willoughby the elder of Wiltshire, but by 1597/8 he was called Thomas Russell of "Aldermaston" or Alderminster, Worcestershire. Here, only four miles south of Stratford, he spent part of his time until after March 13, 1614/15, when John Greene held a court for Russell's manor there. In 1596 he sued for debt a Stratford butcher, William Parry or Perry, who later brought suits against Shakespeare's friends Hamnet Sadler and Richard Tyler. Shakespeare probably knew Russell also in London, where he was arrested about 1599 as surety for Sir George Gifford of Gloucestershire, with whom he had been "bound to go a sea voyage." By this time he was suitor to a widow worth twelve thousand pounds, Mrs. Anne Digges, daughter of Sir Warham St. Leger and widow of Thomas Digges the mathematician. Her London house was in Philip Lane, Aldermanbury, near the houses of Heminge and Condell and Shakespeare's lodging in Silver Street. In 1601 Russell expected to buy, for £3,700, Clopton House near Stratford, with the manor and park, but William Clopton refused to complete the sale. Russell finally married Mrs. Digges in 1603 at Rushock near Droitwich, Worcestershire, and with the aid of the Earl of Devonshire he secured a lease of Rushock from the Merchant Taylors of London. He was described as of Rushock in his mother's will, made in 1607/8, and in a Chancery suit which he brought in 1623 when he was being sued on a bond he had made to a Rushock farmer on November 15, 1615. In 1616 Russell was named an overseer by Shakespeare and in August an executor by his friend John Hanford, esquire, of Eckington near Strensham. Hanford had built a mansion still standing on Bredon Hill, Woolas Hall, with a musicians' gallery and "a rare prospect." He and Russell contributed in 1613 to the buying of new organs for Worcester Cathedral. Russell was a generous friend, for he promised a portion of five hundred pounds for his goddaughter Dorothy Hanford, born in 1614, and bought an estate at Hartlebury for Hanford's son John. He refused to purchase a knighthood from Charles I but he asked his friend Endymion Porter to obtain a baronetcy for his great-nephew Sir William Russell. Thomas Russell of Rushock made his will in 1633, leaving many bequests to friends and most of his estate to Francis Finch, esquire, who proved the will in 1634. Russell's stepson Leonard Digges of Oxford (1588–1635) wrote two poems in praise of Shakespeare.[7]

Francis Collins, the other overseer of Shakespeare's will, was, I find, a member of Clement's Inn. He drew up in 1605 the indentures for Shakespeare's purchase of tithes. At Stratford he served as an attorney in the court of record by 1600, an overseer of the poor in 1602, and a member of the town council from 1602 to 1608. Five of his children were christened or buried at Stratford between 1601 and 1607. Francis Collyns of Clement's Inn was surety in 1607 for John Searson of Tanworth to keep the peace, and his name appears in many other records. From 1609 to 1612 he was the town's solicitor in a suit against Sir Edward Conway, who refused to answer because of the privilege of parliament and then went over the seas to Brill, where he was governor. The corporation wrote about 1614 that Thomas Lucas should acknowledge his wrong done to Mr. Greene and end his suits against Mr. Collins. Collins witnessed deeds of 1605 and 1611 for Sir Edward Greville, in 1607 the will of Nicholas Gibbes of Wilmcote, and in 1610 the deed conveying Hewlands to Bartholomew Hathaway. Thomas Combe's will was witnessed in 1608 by Sir Henry Rainsford, William Barnes, Thomas Greene, and Collins, and the last two witnessed a codicil with John Combe and John Ley. Collins was living at Warwick by 1612/13, when he made the will of John Combe, who left ten pounds to Francis Collins the elder of Warwick, ten marks to his wife Susanna Collins, and ten pounds to their son John, Combe's godson. He was clerk of the peace at Warwick in 1614. Shakespeare's will, which is in his handwriting, left him twenty marks. Francis Collins, gentleman, gave up a house with garden and orchard at the manor court of Henley in October,

1616. He was elected town clerk of Stratford on April 8, 1617, provided he "shall come and dwell amongst us" and serve again as a burgess. The council minutes are in his handwriting from July 17, when he took the oath of office and the oath of supremacy, through September 3, but "M^r ffrancis Collins, steward," was buried at Stratford on September 27, 1617, with the tolling of the great bell. His will, made the day before, left twenty pounds to each of his seven children and to the child "that my wife goeth withall" and divided between Francis and Alice another twenty pounds "that Mr Thomas Combe did promise to give to any of my children."[8]

Shakespeare was friendly with the Combe family, for John Combe left him five pounds and Shakespeare bequeathed "to m^r Thomas Combe my Sword." John was born before 1561 and died on July 10, 1614. Lending money at the usual ten in the hundred made him the richest man in Stratford. Though he sued many debtors, he witnessed the will in 1591 of one man he had sued, Humphrey Brace, a mercer in Chapel Street and town chamberlain, who named as overseers his loving friends Mr. Richard Lane and Mr. John Combe and left each "a Dozen of the best silke poyntes as a token." Combe was chosen by John and Mary Shakespeare in 1598 as a commissioner to examine witnesses. He bought land in Stratford, Old Stratford, and Hampton Lucy in 1594 from Rice Griffin and at Ingon and Hampton Lucy in 1603 from William Clopton, who had already leased Clopton Park to Combe. With his uncle William he sold land in Old Stratford to Shakespeare in 1602. His will, made on January 28, 1612/13, mentioned "Parsons Close alias Shakesperes Close" in Hampton Lucy. His bequests included a hundred pounds for loans to tradesmen, thirty pounds to the poor, and an endowment to pay a learned preacher to make a sermon twice a year in Stratford church. He left sixty pounds for his tomb in the church, more than fifteen hundred pounds in bequests, and the rest of his goods to his nephew Thomas, whom he named executor with Sir Richard Verney of Compton Verney and Bartholomew Hales of Snitterfield.[9]

"An Epitaph upon one Iohn Combe of Stratford upon Aven, a notable Usurer, fastened upon a Tombe that he had caused to be built in his life time" was printed about 1618 in an addition to *Remains after Death* by Richard Brathwaite. Similar verses on an unnamed usurer had been printed in 1608 and 1614, and later manuscripts named three other men as the usurer. Shakespeare was first mentioned as the author in 1634, when Lieutenant Hammond of Norwich wrote that Shakespeare "did merrily fann up some witty, and facetious verses" on "an old Gentleman a Batchelor, Mr Combe." Nicholas Burgh of Windsor heard that Shakespeare wrote on Combe "att his request while hee was yett Liveing" but that after he died, making the poor his heirs, Shakespeare wrote verses praising Combe. Aubrey told a different story, that Shakespeare made the epitaph extempore at a Stratford tavern when Combe was to be buried. Robert Dobyns claimed to have copied the epitaph from the monument in 1673. Shakespeare may have recalled two lines on a usurer and expanded them "merrily" to four lines on "John a Combe."[10]

Thomas Combe, John's brother, lived at the College near the church and held a share in the tithes equal to that of Shakespeare. He married in 1585/6 Mary, widow of William Yonge, sheriff of Shropshire, and died in 1608/9, leaving sons William and Thomas. William (1586–1666/7) studied at Oxford and the Middle Temple, answered Shakespeare in Chancery, and made enclosures at Welcombe, which will be described in the next chapter. The town sent him sack and claret in 1612, gave him the right to build a family pew in the chapel, and sent New Year's gifts to both William and Thomas. William was sheriff of Warwickshire in 1615–16 and captain of the Stratford trained band in 1632, when Leonard Digges wrote that "they say in Stratford that he cannot have less than 20,000[11] in his purse, increased by honest ten and 8 in the hundred." In 1640 he was elected to the Long Parliament, but this election was declared void and he was replaced by a royalist. During the Civil War he mustered militia for the parliamentary army under Lord Brooke and the king's soldiers plundered his house at Stratford. George Willis wrote in 1650, "My uncle Combes is farr in debt and all the land that he hath about Stratford is sould or now upon sale." Of his one son and nine daughters only two daughters survived and had children, Mary, whom John Hall cured when she was a girl of thirteen, and Katherine.[11]

Thomas Combe, the legatee of Shakespeare, was christened on February 9, 1588/9, and entered the Middle Temple in 1608, succeeding with his brother to the chamber of their great-uncle William of Warwick. He lived at Welcombe, and when the Stratford councilors opposed enclosure he called them "doggs & Curres." He was paying tithe-rent in 1615 to Greene, who heard a story of "his kickyng & beatyng his sheppard at Meon demandyng his wages" and wrote in 1616 of Thomas Combe and Valentine Tant of Henley Street "fightyng at Bishopton." Though he was presented in 1621 and 1622 for not receiving the sacrament at Easter, he took part in electing churchwardens and his will shows that he was a Protestant, like the rest of the Combes. William and Thomas were listed in 1640–41 as subsidy men, not as recusants. Thomas held office under the Commonwealth as sheriff of Warwickshire in 1648 and as recorder of Stratford from 1648 till his death in 1657. His will left land for gowns for the poor, two sermons a year, and a yearly feast for the corporation. Since he had never married, he made bequests to his loving kinsman Mr. George Willis of Fenny Compton (son of George Willis, governor of Connecticut, who had married Combe's half-sister Bridget Yonge at Stratford in 1609) and to his ancient acquaintance and trusty friend Mr. John Washington of Shottery (a cousin of Colonel John Washington of Virginia).[12]

Shakespeare remembered in his will Mr. Anthony Nash of Welcombe and his brother Mr. John Nash. Both witnessed the Combes' deed to Shakespeare in 1602, and Anthony witnessed agreements by Shakespeare in 1605 and 1614. Their father Thomas Nash, whose mother was a Hubaud, had gathered tithes for Sir John Hubaud. Ralph Hubaud and Anthony Nash of Welcombe bought part of Sir John's lease in 1588 and sold it in 1599 to Sir

Edward Greville, whom Nash sued in 1615 in the court of Requests. Nash was farmer for Shakespeare's tithes in 1606 and 1614. He also bought land from Rice Griffin which he sold in 1616 to Julines Shaw. In the same year Sir William Somerville died owing him one hundred and five pounds. Commissioners on the enclosure in 1617 accepted the testimony of Anthony Nash, gentleman, "which hath knowne the Customes there above ffortie yeares, and to whose indifferency" the townsmen and William Combe referred themselves. The heralds in 1619 recorded him as a gentleman, and he paid more subsidy than any man in the parish except William and Thomas Combe. When he died in 1622 he left six hundred pounds and plate to his wife Mary, five hundred pounds to his younger son John, and "that little land I have," the Bear Inn and another house in Bridge Street and the Butt Close by the Avon, to his son Thomas (1593–1647), who studied at Lincoln's Inn and married Shakespeare's granddaughter in 1626.[13]

Anthony's brother John Nash, who died in 1623, had a wife Elizabeth (d. 1597) and a second wife Dorothy (d. 1621), whose first husband was Francis Bellars, vintner (d. 1602). His sons by his first wife were Anthony, John, and Thomas, and by his second, Francis, aged fourteen in 1619, and William, christened on June 20, 1611. John Nash of Stratford on Avon, gentleman, was sued in Queen's Bench for trespass in Easter term, 1588, and in Michaelmas term Richard Quiney sought sureties of the peace against him. The Bear Inn, whose host had been Francis Bellars, was kept in the name of John Nash, but it was probably managed by his servant Thomas Jeffs, presented in 1603/4 for making malt, and his wife Dorothy Nash, presented in 1606 for keeping unlawful games. The town paid him in 1614 for a dinner for Sir William Somerville and paid Mrs. Nash in 1616 "for a banket," and John Hall later treated one of Nash's servants at the Bear. Like Shakespeare, Nash held tithes under the lease to Sir John Hubaud. In 1609 he wrote to Thomas Greene, "wee that hold of the same lease will contribute to the charge" of buying the rent due to Barker, and asked Greene to consult at the Bull's Head in Paul's Chain with

Mr. Clarke of Herefordshire, who lately "lay at my house." Richard Clerke and Thomas Nash had been trustees for Hubaud. John Nash opposed the vicar in 1619 and was sued in Star Chamber. The attorney general described him as the leader of rioters who threatened to flay Mr. Wilson in the church, crying out "hange him, kill him, pull out his throate," and who devised rhymes which they read and sang in taverns and alehouses.[14]

Shakespeare left money for a ring to William Reynolds, gentleman. Reynolds (1575–1632/3) gave arms of three foxes' heads in 1619 as son and heir of Thomas Reynolds and grandson of Hugh Reynolds, bailiff of Stratford College and one of the original aldermen of the town. Thomas lived in Chapel Street and at Colles Farm in Old Stratford near the church. He and his wife were recusants in 1592, and in 1603/4 a "supposed Semynary escaped at Stratford," wearing green breeches, high shoes, and white stockings, was seen running from the gild hall to Mr. Reynolds's door in Chapel Street. When Thomas died in September, 1613, one "Willyam Raynoules of Stretfard" was in prison at Warwick, but this may have been another William who kept an alehouse in Church Street. In 1615 Thomas's son William proved the will of his mother Margaret, who left most of her estate to her "welbeloved sonne William Raynoldes," with twenty pounds each to six other children. John Hall and John Greene were witnesses and overseers, and other witnesses were William Barnes of Clifford Chambers and Alderman Barber. She asked to be buried in the chancel near her husband. William inherited her land in Welcombe and the grounds called Salmon Jole and Salmon Tail near the College, which John Combe had left to his cousin Mrs. Reynolds and then to William. Combe had given all his plate and household goods to Mrs. Reynolds, and these also came to William. Three months after his mother's death he married, on August 3, 1615, at Clifford Chambers, Frances de Bois "of London in Phillip Lane. French." Their daughter Anne was christened in 1618, Elinor in 1620, and another Elinor in 1622. A Star Chamber bill charged John Nash, William Reynolds, and others with riot and libel in 1619 against the new vicar and other Puritans and with setting up again the Maypole in Church Way, near the house of Reynolds. He answered that his name had been inserted "uppon some causles mallice" and that he was not guilty of the misdemeanors as set forth. In 1621 he was an assessor of subsidy and one of the chief landowners in Old Stratford. His widow married in 1636 Mr. Richard Wright, the former assistant schoolmaster from Oxford, who was minister at Bishopton in 1614, at Luddington in 1617, and at Billesley in 1619. Elinor, daughter and heiress of William Reynolds of Shottery, married Edward Carew, nephew of the poet Thomas Carew.[15]

Mr. Richard Tyler the elder was given a ring in the first draft of Shakespeare's will, but in the final draft he was replaced by Hamnet Sadler. As will be seen in the next chapter, he was charged in 1615/16 with failing to account for money which he had collected. He was probably at school with Shakespeare, since he was born in 1566, the son of William Tyler, butcher and alderman, for whom Shakespeare's father had acted as chamberlain. Richard volunteered to serve as a soldier in the year of the Armada, when the town paid William Baynton and Richard Tyler "for ther swordes & daggers." Against her father's wish he married Susanna, daughter of Richard Woodward of Shottery Manor, gentleman. Her rich grandfather, Robert Perrott, left her out of his will in March 1588/9 and warned her sisters not to match themselves without the consent of their parents. In 1590 Alderman Hill left a bequest to Tyler and the council chose him a member, at the unusually early age of twenty-four, but he resigned in 1594. His children included Richard, born in 1592, Judith in 1593, Susanna in 1597, and William in 1598. In the malt returns of 1595 and 1598 he was "Mr Richard Tyler" of Sheep Street. In 1607 the constables presented "m^r Richard Tyler for a ffray on m^r Lucas, & he, on m^r Tyler." Lucas and Francis Collins as commissioners signed the answer of Tyler in 1608 to a bill in the court of Requests brought by John Browne of Stratford, gentleman. Browne declared that, intending to make a voyage to Rome, he sold his gelding to Tyler for a bond to pay twice its value when he returned (the wager implying that there was an even chance of his not returning) but that since he was "altogether unlearned" he took the bond before having it read to him and then found that it was for fourteen pounds instead of the thirty-two pounds he had expected. Tyler answered that Browne was "a manne of a turbulent spiritte and much inclyned to a trowblesome kinde of lieffe," that he agreed to pay twice what the horse should be judged worth by George Perry and John Tomlins (neither he nor Browne to know the price until the bond was sealed), and that Perry and Tomlins priced the horse at twenty nobles (less than seven pounds) which was all it was worth, not sixteen pounds. Perry agreed with Tyler. His brother William Perry, butcher, had Tyler bound over to keep the peace in 1612, but the town council described William as "A man of an evill wicked and Contencious spiritt" and petitioned the lord chancellor to discharge "Richard Tyler gentleman a man of honest Conversacion & quiet & peaceable Carryage amongst his neighbours & towardes all people." William Perry had been suspected of coining gold. After losses in the fire of 1614, Tyler was authorized to collect contributions in Kent. His signature appears on a deed in 1617/18 transferring Shakespeare's house in Blackfriars, the same signature found in a lease of 1604 from Sir George and Lady Carew. He was a churchwarden in 1621, as his son Richard was in 1625. Mr. Richard Tyler, gentleman, died in 1636.[16]

Hamnet Sadler inherited copyhold from Henry Sadler, probably his father, and was heir to his kinsman Roger Sadler, baker and former bailiff. Sadlers had lived in Stratford since the reign of Richard II. By his will in 1578, which mentioned debts of John Shakespeare and Richard Hathaway, Roger left to Hamnet three houses in Church Street and the lease of his dwelling in High Street after the death of his wife Margaret, who died in 1595. Hamnet married before 1580 a wife named Judith, said to have been Judith Staunton, and had fourteen children, seven of whom died young. Shakespeare's twins were named Hamnet and Judith, and the Sadlers named a son William in 1597/8. When a suit between Sadler and Ananias Nason was settled in 1584, the town paid for sack and claret for the arbiters, Sir Thomas Lucy and Sir Fulke Greville. Sadler was chosen constable in 1593. The return of maltsters in 1595 reported that "Hamlett Sadler usethe onlye his bakers trade," with a household of six, and he was presented with other bakers several times, in 1603/4 for some breach of the statute on baking household bread and cakes. He never recovered financially from his losses in the fire of 1595, though he rebuilt his house at the corner of High Street and Sheep Street, "next the Corn Market." After buying the right to gather money by patent in Wiltshire, in order to travel he hired a mare for twenty-four days at a shilling a day, for which he was sued by John Lupton. In 1597 he and Quiney spent three months "in the collectinge of Suffolke and Norfolk." "I would Hamlet weare at home," Sturley wrote of this journey, "freed from further travell." Another year he wrote, "Judith Sadler waxeth very heavy for the burden of her childing and also of the want of her husband," and wished that Quiney would send him home from London with money in his purse. Sadler was often sued for debt in the court of record, as in 1601 for money due for wheat to William Walford and to the vicar, Richard Byfield. In that year he witnessed the will of his sister's husband, John Smith, vintner, who left his "brother Hamlet Sadler" his gown, black doublet, and hat lined with velvet. In 1606 the will of Helen, sister of Roger Sadler and widow of a rich vintner in London, Stephen Scudamore of St. Stephen, Coleman Street, forgave "my cousin Hamlett Sadler all suche debtes as he oweth me by bondes" and left a featherbed and bolster to his daughter Margaret. John Combe sued Sadler on a bond made in 1611/12. Sadler's house was "muche outt of repaire" in 1613, and he sold the lease after Judith died the next year. He witnessed Shakespeare's will and lived until 1624.[17]

Another witness to Shakespeare's will was Mr. July Shaw, who lived in the second house from Shakespeare's in Chapel Street. He signed his first name "July," "Julynes," "Julyns," and "Julyne,"

and in Latin records it was "Julianus" and "Julinus." He was
"July" in the records of his christening in 1571, of his marriage
in 1594 to Anne, widow of Arthur Boyes, and of his burial in
1629. Shakespeare's father in 1592 priced the goods of Ralph
Shaw, wool-driver, who left his son July forty pounds. In 1595 it
was reported that "Julye Shawe usethe the trades of buyinge and
sellinge of woll and yorne. And malltinge," and he was sued on the
statute for trading in wool in 1593 and 1600. He was prosperous
enough to pay subsidy by 1605. His house near New Place, with
barn and garden, was leased in 1597 to Julinus Shawe, yeoman,
but in 1613 to Julins Shawe, gentleman. He bought property in
1602 from Elizabeth Quiney and in later years from William
Smith, Anthony Nash, and William Chandler. After he had served
as churchwarden, burgess, and chamberlain, the council made special mention in 1613 that "The Aldermen, much approvyng his
well-deservynges in this place, have, for his honesty, fidelity, and
good opinion of him, chosen Julins Shawe to be an Alderman." He
was bailiff when he witnessed Shakespeare's will in 1616, and
served again in 1627–1628.[18]

Mr. Thomas Greene of the Middle Temple was living at New
Place in 1609, and in 1614 and 1615 he wrote of "my Cosen
Shakespear." His first children baptized at Stratford, where he became town clerk in 1603, were named Anne in 1603/4 and William in 1607/8. He and Shakespeare may have been kinsmen by
blood or they may have been connections by marriage. He informed
the heralds in 1623 that his grandfather Oliver Greene of Tanworth had married Joan Fetherstone, that his father Thomas of
Warwick had married Isabel, daughter of Henry Lingen, and that
he had married Lettice, daughter of Henry Tutt of West Meon,
Hampshire. Oliver of Tanworth made a will in 1545 bequeathing
his books to his son Thomas, and Thomas of Warwick, mercer, in
1590 left eighty pounds and a grey mare to his son Thomas and a
house in Northampton to his son John, who also settled in Stratford. Thomas, son and heir of Thomas Greene of Warwick, gentleman, deceased, entered the Middle Temple in 1595 from Staple

Inn on the surety of John Marston of Coventry and his son John, later the dramatist. Greene afterwards gave surety for William Somerville and other students, all from Warwickshire or Gloucestershire. He was solicitor for Stratford in 1601, consulting Sir Edward Coke, and the next year he was called to the bar.[19]

A Thomas Greene welcomed King James with a poem in 1603, *A Poets Vision and a Princes Glorie,* and wrote a sonnet to Drayton which appeared in the 1603 edition of *The Barons' Wars.* Drayton's latest editors believe that the author was probably Shakespeare's "cousin." This is not certain, but it seems a reasonable conjecture. Drayton had many friends at the Temple, including John and Francis Beaumont and John Selden of the Inner Temple and Sir Henry Goodere the younger, George Sandys, and Henry Lucas of the Middle Temple. He often visited Sir Henry Rainsford, who entered the Middle Temple in 1594, and Thomas Greene of Stratford gave surety for the younger Henry Rainsford, admitted in 1616. Both Greene and the Rainsfords claimed descent from the Greenes of Green's Norton, Northamptonshire. Among Greene's papers at Stratford are Latin verses and a few jottings in his hand such as "Love is not to be so suppresed with Wisdom. Because ytt cannot be Comprehend With Resone Love is a s. . . . . thing. Cause a Lover Loveth his Torment." Drayton's friend also modernized the English in a prose translation of *The History of the Seven Wise Maisters,* which had been printed by Pynson in 1493, by Wynkyn de Worde in 1520, and by William Copland about 1555. In an edition of 1602 at the Huntington Library, not recorded in the *Short-Title Catalogue* but called to my attention by Franklin B. Williams, Jr., an epistle by "Thomas Greene G[entle]man to the learned Reader" explains that the printer had asked him to correct "the phrase and penning," since they differed from "the ancient phrase" of Chaucer which "may be permitted for a monument of antiquitie."[20]

Greene was steward and town clerk of Stratford from 1603 to 1617, living in 1609 at New Place and by 1611 at St. Mary's House near the church. Three of his children were baptized at

Stratford and three others were buried there between 1604 and 1615. One of his duties as counsel for the town was to negotiate in London for a new charter, which was finally granted in 1610. He was steward of Throckmorton manor and of other manors for Thomas Throckmorton, and Sir Edward Conway paid him a yearly fee for his counsel. He joined Richard Lane and Shakespeare in their Chancery suit after buying a lease of tithes in 1609 from Humphrey Colles of the Middle Temple. The corporation took notice in 1610 that Mr. Greene "standeth secretlie scandalized and uniustly sklaundred bie unknowen aucthores, That he hath hearetofore deceaved and dealt evillie with us in buyinge of one Humfrie Coles esquier an intereste in tithes the inheritance wheareof is in us," but certified that the charge was false and that he "for his fidelitie and endevors in our behalfes allwaies used us verie well." They sent a pottle of claret the next year "to Mr. Greens to a gentilman of London their." When they resolved in 1614 to resist the enclosure at Welcombe, they secured Greene's written declaration of his purpose "as the Steward & Counsellour of the sayd Borough to assist them agaynst the sayd inclosure." As will be seen in the next chapter, he carried out this promise faithfully until he resigned and was succeeded by Francis Collins on April 8, 1617. Having decided to leave Stratford, he offered to sell for two hundred and eighty pounds St. Mary's House, "A pretty neate gentleman like howse with a pretty garden and a lyttle yonge Orchard standinge very Sweete and quiett the place and buildinge within this .6. yeres Cost above. 400^{li}," and he asked five hundred and ninety pounds for his lease of tithes. When Sir Henry Rainsford proposed that he accept two hundred and forty pounds for the house and four hundred pounds for the tithes, Greene agreed, though he wrote that he deserved "recompense to a greater value for my golden dayes and spirites spent in Stratfordes Service." He received part of the money in June, 1617, warranting possession of the house against any claim in his right or that of his wife, her cousin Sir Alexander Tutt, or her brother Chidiock Tutt. The rest he arranged to be paid in February, "xl^l to m^r Hall at Newplace" and other sums "to m^r Collyns there," "to me at m^r Halles at Newplace," to Sir Robert Lee at Billesley, to Mr. Timothy Wagstaff at Warwick, and to Sir Henry Rainsford at Clifford. Greene was chosen reader at the Middle Temple in 1621, when his son William was admitted, and he became a master of the bench and treasurer. He lived at Bristol until 1640, when his will left most of his estate "unto Lettice, my most dear and loving wife, being sorry that I have no more to leave to so good a woman." She proved the will on July 1, 1641.[21]

Greene's brother, John Greene of Clement's Inn, became a trustee of Shakespeare's house in Blackfriars in 1617/18, acting for Susanna Hall. Born about 1575, he was attorney for Hamnet Sadler at Stratford in 1599. After marrying Margaret Lane in 1609, he was appointed an attorney of the court of record in 1611, solicitor for town causes at London or elsewhere in 1612, and a deputy town clerk in 1613. In 1612 he sued John Browne, gentleman, for his attorney's fees. He served on the council as a chief burgess from 1612 to June, 1615, when he went to dwell for a time at Bidford. Shakespeare's friend Thomas Russell employed him as steward at a manor court for Alderminster held in 1614/15. Mrs. Reynolds made John Hall and John Greene overseers of her will on May 2, 1615, and in September Thomas Greene wrote down what Shakespeare had said to John Greene about the enclosure. Lord Carew recommended John Greene for town clerk in May, 1617, but Collins had already been chosen. Greene testified for the corporation in 1635, giving his age as threescore, and he died at Stratford in 1640.[22]

CHAPTER IX

THE LAST YEARS

❖After he finished writing *The Tempest* in 1611, Shakespeare was probably free to spend most of his time at Stratford. His presence there happens to be recorded in September, 1611, October, 1614, September, 1615, and March and April, 1616. He testified in the court of Requests at Westminster on May 11, 1612, but was not examined on June 19 as had been intended, so that by then he had probably returned to Stratford. In March, 1612/13, he signed documents in London for his purchase of the Blackfriars gatehouse and in the same month devised for the Earl of Rutland an impresa, or emblem and motto for a shield, which was painted by Richard Burbage. Thomas Greene wrote at London on November 17, 1614, of "my Cosen shakespeare commyng yesterday to towne," with John Hall, and Shakespeare was still away from home at Christmas.[1]

Thomas Greene was living at New Place in 1609 with his wife and two children, Anne and William. He was waiting to move into St. Mary's House, then occupied by George Browne. On September 9, 1609, he delivered to Sir Henry Rainsford "some reasons to prove that G. Browne ment before this to have bene gone." After mentioning that he had pulled down the walnut trees in Lent by the good liking of Browne, Greene wrote: "he doubted whether he might sowe his garden, untill about my going to the Terme (seing I could gett no carryage to help me here with tymber) I was content to permytt yt without contradicion. & the rather because

I perceyved I might stay another yere at new place." Greene appealed to the arbiters: "I desire I may have the possession at our Lady Day next that I may begyn to make yt reddy agaynst michaelmas next." He may not have gained possession until 1611, for when he offered the house for sale in May, 1617, he said that it had cost him above four hundred pounds "within this .6. yeres." In June, 1611, the corporation promised "to repare the Church yeard wall at m^r Greens dwelling house." Shakespeare and Greene both contributed in September towards the cost of prosecuting a bill in parliament for the better repair of highways. Judith Shakespeare joined Thomas Greene and his wife Lettice, on December 4, in witnessing a deed made by Elizabeth Quiney and her son Adrian.[2]

Greene had a patent as steward of the borough in 1603, and from that year until 1617, except when he was at London for the terms, he kept most of the minutes for the council meetings at the gild hall. The council voted in 1611 that he might make Mr. Sturley or Mr. John Greene his deputy for keeping the court of record in his absence and that half the profits of the court belonged to the town clerk and his deputy. The Council Book furnishes glimpses of life in Stratford during Shakespeare's last years. Thirty alehouses were to be allowed in the town, and three inns, the Crown, Bear, and Swan, all in Bridge Street. The Bailiff for 1610–11, William Walford, was granted the toll from strangers at fairs and markets: a penny from the buyer and a penny from the seller for every score of sheep bought, sold, or exchanged, and for every "beast," bull, or boar. A servant named Joan refused to serve her master because "she was once frighted in the night in the Chamber where her maisters late wief dyed but by what or whom she cannot tell"; she was sent to prison until she would serve. William Slatter confessed "that he marryed himself in his Chamber no body else being by & hopeth that maryage to be lawfull," but he hoped in vain and had to marry again in the church. Thomas Gardener claimed to have been married in an alehouse at Haselor by "Sr Roger of Preston." The penalty for breaking the order against plays imposed in 1602 was increased in 1611/12 from ten shillings to ten pounds. The order of 1602 had provided "that there shalbe no plays or enterlewedes playd in the Chamber, the guild halle, nor in any parte of the howsse or Courte ffrom hensforward." When the King's Men came to Stratford for the first time in 1622, they were given money but were not allowed to play.[3]

Shakespeare contributed in 1611 "towardes the Charge of prosecutynge the Bill in parliament for the better Repayre of the highe waies and amendinge divers defectes in the Statutes alredy made." The list of contributors drawn up on September 11 is headed by the chief alderman, the steward ("m^r Thomas Greene esquire—ij^s vj^d"), and the other aldermen, and the next name, added in the margin, is that of "m^r William shackspere." Of seventy-one names in the list, the only others called "master" besides those mentioned are Robert Butler, John Lane, John and William Combe, Richard Tyler, John Nash, and John Hall. The justices of the peace may have spoken of the need for such a bill when they surveyed the highway in Bridgetown this year and were feasted with wine, sugar, pippins, and beer. An inventory of the goods of Robert Johnson, vintner, written by Mr. Aspinall the schoolmaster on October 5, 1611, included "A lease of a barne that he holdeth of Mr Shaxper, xx^{li}." Johnson had lived in Henley Street since 1591, keeping an inn later called the White Lion. Shakespeare's granddaughter in her will of 1670 mentioned this barn as held by Michael Johnson and belonging to her houses in Henley Street, and it was described in 1730 as situated in the Gild Pits, near the back gates of the Swan Inn.[4]

Master Rogers the vicar became Shakespeare's neighbor in 1611, when he and his family moved to the old Priest's House within the chapel precinct. He was probably the "Jo: Rogers" who signed the agreement between Shakespeare and Replingham in 1614. The chamberlains paid Rogers at Whitsuntide, 1608, "for the sermon of remembrance for Mr. Perrot" and in 1615 for three special sermons, while in 1616 they sent wine to Mr. Rogers when his brother preached. The council voted in April, 1614, to lease the churchyard

to Rogers, for his own use to pasture "fit cattle," so long as he
acknowledged the corporation's right to the churchyard according to
the arbitrament of Sir Fulke Greville and others. They refused his
request to have "a plecke of grownd in Schollers Lane," "to keepe a
swine or two in," but allowed him to build a stable for his horse
and a "fewell house." In 1615 they entreated Mr. Rogers the minister to persuade Mr. Combe, and the bailiff wrote the next year of
"the mynysters Threatnyngs against Enclosures." Although they decided that he should not have any more benefit from the burials,
since the fees were needed to repair the church and chancel, they
made him a gift of a furred gown in 1618 "in hope that hee will
well deserve the same hereafter: And amend his former faultes and
faylinges." A clue to these may be found in the will of Francis
Collins, who wrote that he and Rogers were trustees of a legacy of
two houses left for the poor but that Rogers and Thomas Lucas
"did combyne themselves togeather and keepe it from the poore
most uncontionably." Rogers was removed as vicar in 1619 on the
ground that he had obtained another benefice. Lord Chancellor
Verulam presented Thomas Wilson, whose coming led to a riot and
the writing of a "sonnett" imagined as spoken by Rogers:

> Revenge still brother Rogers shall not live,
> maye I not live, o whoe will with mee mourne . . .
> the feyned freinds, with feyned lookes betraye,
> Baker had never lived to vanquish me,
> Had it not bene for Lucas trecherye.

The Star Chamber bill against John Nash, William Reynolds, and
others quoted also "A Satyre to the Cheife rulers in the Synagogue
of Stratford," seven Puritans:

> A heavy curse (o lord) upon them send
> because they have bereft us of our best friende,

who was John Rogers.[5]
   The corporation sent New Year's gifts to Lady Greville, wife of
Sir Edward, a keg of sturgeon in 1609 and a sugar loaf in 1611. A
"gratuity" of twenty cheeses bought from Mr. Nash was given in

1614 to the high steward, Lord Carew of Clopton, and six fat
wethers in 1617 to the recorder, Sir Fulke Greville of Warwick
Castle, who sent venison for the bailiff's feast, as in 1613 when he
gave a buck from Wedgnock Park and in 1615 one from Beauchamp's Court. With a present of "a good sugar loafe & Wyne" in
October, 1614, Master Bailiff and all the company entertained Lord
Compton, who became Earl of Northampton and president of
Wales and chose John Hall for his physician. In the same year Sir
Fulke Greville was an arbiter between the vicar and the corporation, and the town paid "for one quart of sack and one quart of
clarrett winne geven to a precher at the newe place." This preacher
had probably come to deliver the Hamlet Smith sermon at Easter or
the Perrott sermon at Whitsuntide, since the payment appears between entries dated March 21 and June 30, 1614. About September
the town paid "the chargies of mr beck when he preched here."
Preachers were often invited to give special sermons at the chapel,
and New Place was just across the way.[6]

While Shakespeare was living in Stratford, on July 9, 1614, the
town suffered its third great fire. Preachers had made much of the
fact that the fires of 1594 and 1595 broke out on Sunday. Thomas
Beard wrote in *The Theatre of Gods Judgements* (1597), "and
that which is most strange within these late yeres, a whole town
hath bene twise burnt, for the breach of the Sabbath by the inhabitants," adding in 1612, "as all men judged." Lewis Bayly, preaching at Evesham in 1611, explained that "*Stratford* upon *Avon* was
twice on the same day twelvemoneth (being the Lords Day) almost
consumed with fire: chiefly for prophaning the *Lords Sabbaths,* and
for contemning his word in the mouth of his faithfull *Ministers.*"
Unluckily the fire of 1614 came on a Saturday. Sir Fulke and Sir
Edward Greville, William Combe, and other justices certified that
this "suddaine and terrible Fire" burnt fifty-four houses, with
barns, stables, grain, hay, and timber, worth eight thousand pounds;
"the force of which fire was so great (the wind sitting full uppon
the Towne) that it dispersed into so many places therof whereby
the whole Towne was in very great daunger to have been utterly

consumed." The council ordered more buckets, spouts, fire hooks, and ladders, and petitioned the lord chief justice to forbid thatched houses, for "the wynde taketh the Thatch & carryeth it very farr of and there fireth other Thatched howses," so that "very many fayer tyled howses have byn burned to the ground." A royal patent granted on December 5, printed by Thomas Purfoot, authorized William Wyatt, Richard Tyler, and three others to gather contributions for the sufferers from fire. Sir Richard Verney, Sir Henry Rainsford, and Bartholomew Hales, who examined the collectors' accounts in March, 1615/16, found "every one prefferinge his owne private benifittes befor the generall good" and "exhibitinge to us bills of Charges, excedinge theare Collectiones." Tyler petitioned the lord chancellor, offering to account for his collections, but another petition in the hand of Thomas Greene charged Tyler with being "unreasonably slack" and refusing to yield an account. He was not reappointed when a second patent was granted on May 11, 1616; but by June he reported collections of one hundred and twenty-three pounds in Kent. In September the commissioners and the corporation approved agreements that Mr. Tyler "shall Collect the Countie of Kent . . . to his owne use" and that Wyatt and the rest should collect in other counties and the University of Cambridge. The criticism of Tyler in 1615/16 may explain why Shakespeare removed Tyler's name from his will.[7]

Shakespeare did not share the concern of the town council over a plan to enclose fields at Welcombe. William Replingham agreed on October 28, 1614, to recompense him for all loss by "inclosure or decaye of tyllage," since sheep pastures would pay less in tithes than fields of grain and hay. Replingham, an attorney, was acting for his cousin Arthur Mainwaring, steward to Lord Chancellor Ellesmere. Shakespeare's lawyer, Thomas Lucas of Stratford and Gray's Inn, also safeguarded the rights of Thomas Greene, who had a lease of the other half of the tithes, and Greene mentioned other covenants with Mrs. Reynolds and "at first with Arthur Cawdrey." Greene noted on September 5 that the enclosure would not affect Shakespeare's freehold, and Shakespeare told him on November 16

"that they meane in Aprill to survey the Land & then to gyve satis-
faccion & not before: & he and m^r Hall say they think ther will be
nothyng done at all." A survey, however, was made in December,
when Greene tried to find Replingham at the Bear and at New
Place. He and the town authorities urged William Combe at the
College not enclose, but Combe answered "that indeed he was to
have some profytt by the Inclosure" but that the enclosure was for
Mr. Mainwaring and that "the Company hadd by styrrynge in this
busynes gott he would not say the greatest, but almost the greatest
men of England to be our enemyes." A threat to have the lord
chancellor write to the town was not carried out. The town council
wrote letters on December 23 to Mr. Mainwaring and to Mr. Shakespeare, and Greene "also wrytt of myself to my Cosen Shakspear."
On the same day the council sought support from Andrew Archer
of Tanworth, who owned Bishopton manor and common in the
intended enclosure, and Sir Francis Smith, who had land at Welcombe. Lord Carew of Clopton had already said that he meant to
oppose the enclosing "all he might," and Lord Compton was reminded of "his promise to the Countrey at the last dyggynge" (in
1607, when "the diggers of Warwickshire" had risen against enclosures).[8]

On advice of Greene, William Walford and William Chandler
became tenants at Welcombe by buying a lease on January 6, 1615.
Three days later they went with spades to fill in a ditch being dug
for a hedge, but Combe had his diggers throw them to the ground
while he "sat laughing on his horsback & sayd they wer good foot-
ball playres." He also called them "puritan knaves & underlings in
their colour" (pretence, referring to the legal strategy by which the
two townsmen had acquired rights as commoners). He offered
Greene ten pounds "to propound a peace," but Greene remained
loyal to the corporation. Women and children filled in the ditches
the next day. The council urged Replingham to entreat Mainwaring
to forbear, asked Mr. Rogers the vicar to persuade Combe not to
enclose, and declared that the enclosers had broken their former
agreements. After considering a Star Chamber suit to prevent en-

closure and punish riots, the council petitioned Chief Justice Coke, who ordered a stay of enclosure. Mainwaring gave up, but Combe questioned Coke's authority, beat and imprisoned tenants, and depopulated the whole village of Welcombe except his own house. He told Arthur Cawdrey "that yf he sowed his said wheat land he would eate yt vpp with his sheepe." Greene noted in September, 1615, "W Shakespeares tellyng J Greene that I was not able to beare the encloseinge of Welcombe." What this means is not clear, but he first wrote "to he" (perhaps starting to write "to help" and then seeing that this could be taken in two ways, "to remedy" or "to aid") and he may have intended to write "to barre." At the Lent assizes in 1616 Coke forbore to punish Combe because he was then high sheriff but "badd him sett his hart at rest he should never enclose nor lay downe his Common errable land soelong as he [Coke] served the King." Combe made new proposals in April and June, but the council answered that they desired no enclosure or innovation. The bailiff wrote in December that Combe's conscience was "blinded as yt seemeth with a desire to make your self Riche by other mens losse," so that he paid no heed to the charges of judges "nor the mynysters Threatnyngs against Enclosures." When the bailiff sued him in 1617, he pocketed up the warrant delivered him by Richard Hathaway, Mrs. Shakespeare's nephew. After Greene had drawn up many petitions, the privy council ordered Combe in 1619 to remove all enclosures made against the orders of the judges of assize.[9]

John Marston the dramatist had been a surety with his father in 1595 for the admission of Thomas Greene to the Middle Temple. The Stratford records preserve the copy of a letter to Marston, not signed or addressed but dated from Stratford on February 24, 1615/16:

These are to scertifie you that the bearer hereof Arthure Brogden of Stratford uppon Avon in the Countie of Warwick butcher our honest neighboure sonne of Thomas Brogden late of Stratford aforesaid draper decessed Which Thomas Brogden in his Lyfe Tyme delivered into the haundes of Mr Marston late of the Cytie of Coventrie de-

cessed your late ffather scertaine Evidences, for the drawinge of certaine
Conveyances betwixt him the said Thomas Brogden and others Which
said Evidences, as wee are geven to understand after the decesse of
your ffather came unto youre handes as Executor to youre ffather) Our
yernest request is to intreate youre ffrendshipp that you Wilbe plesed
to steede this bearer in Lokinge upp of the said Evidences and de-
liveringe of them unto him, Who shall not onlie thinke him selfe
gretlie beholdinge unto you, butt also give you anye resonable con-
tente for youre paynes, And Wee our selves Whose names are under
wrytten, shalbe as redye to doe you the like pleasure yf you have
occasion to use us in Warwickeshere, and soe doe rest
                                          Youre Lovinge ffrendes.

The letter sent to Marston was presumably signed by the bailiff,
who was July Shaw, and other aldermen. Perhaps Greene knew
where to find Marston in London, where he was robbed in August,
1616, or at Barford in Wiltshire, where he was then a clergyman.
Thomas Brogden, host of the King's Hall tavern, served on the
council from 1571 to 1581, and his son Arthur was born in 1586.
Among the Charlecote manuscripts is a conveyance of Sandbarn
Farm in 1575 by Thomas Brogden, draper; and his widow Alice,
who died in 1615, had inherited property from her father, Alderman Perrott. The elder Marston was counsel for the town in a law-
suit of 1590.[10]

Shakespeare's daughter Judith married Thomas Quiney at Stratford church on February 10, 1615/16. They were summoned to appear before the consistory court in Worcester Cathedral for marrying without a license. Quiney, cited by Nixon, did not appear and
was excommunicated. Whether the same sentence was given against
Judith is not clear, for the last word of the record is not "vxor" but
"exco" for "excommunicatio" or "excommunicatus." Their marriage had probably been by banns, since they were not cited for
marrying without banns or license, as another Stratford man was in
May, 1616. Although marriage by banns was proper at most times
of the year, a license should have been secured for marriage between
Septuagesima Sunday and the Sunday after Easter, from January 28
to April 7 in 1616. The Stratford clergy, however, often celebrated

marriages during February, recording three in the register for this year, signed by Richard Watts, assistant minister, who married Quiney's sister in 1623. The Quineys may have been summoned only because the summoner saw a chance to collect a fee. William Nixon, the summoner or apparitor, got into trouble and was himself excommunicated. According to the attorney general's bill in Star Chamber, he took bribes in 1617 to discharge offenders "of his own head and authority" and in 1619 "subtlely forged" an injunction against John Pinke, counterfeiting the name of William Warmestrey, register of the consistory court. Thomas Russell named Warmestrey a trustee in 1617 and left Mrs. Warmestrey "my pointed Diamond Ring." Quiney did not long remain excommunicated, for in November, 1616, his son Shakespeare was baptized in the church.[11]

Judith Shakespeare signed twice by mark as witness in 1611 to a deed of Elizabeth Quiney and her son Adrian. Thomas Quiney, born in 1589, was managing his mother's business by 1608, when he sold wine to the corporation. He leased in 1611 the tavern next door to his mother's house in High Street, but he and Judith moved in July, 1616, to the Cage, at the corner of High Street and Bridge Street. Shakespeare, son of Thomas Quiney, gentleman, was christened on November 23, but the "great bell" tolled for him on May 8, 1617; and his brothers Richard, born in 1618, and Thomas, born in 1620, both died in 1639. Thomas Quiney was chosen burgess and constable in 1617 and chamberlain in 1621 and 1622, heading his second account with a couplet in French from the poet Saint-Gelais. About 1630 he paid small fines, like many others, for swearing and for allowing tippling, engaged in a lawsuit over wine he had bought at Bristol, and tried to sell his lease of the Cage. The lease was made over in trust for his wife and sons in 1633 to his kinsmen John Hall, Thomas Nash, and Richard Watts, and in 1652 to his brother Richard. He was still selling wine to the corporation in 1650, and there is no evidence that he ever left Stratford. Nash in 1647 bequeathed rings to Thomas and Judith Quiney, and Richard Quiney in 1655 bequeathed his brother an annuity. Judith, wife of Thomas Quiney, gentleman, died in 1661/2 at the age of seventy-seven. Thomas may have died in 1662 or 1663, when there is a gap in the register.[12]

Shakespeare's last will and testament is dated March 25, 1616. Francis Collins wrote the document, since the handwriting matches exactly his handwriting in the Council Book. Collins may have prepared a draft in January, for when he wrote a new first sheet on March 25 he wrote "Januarij" and then corrected it to "martij." He did not recopy the second and third sheets, but Shakespeare had him make many changes and additions. Shakespeare left all his houses and lands to Susanna, entailed upon her eldest son or heir male and then upon the heirs male of Judith. John and Susanna Hall, the executors, were to have all the personal property not otherwise bequeathed. Judith, whose marriage to Thomas Quincy in February was not mentioned, was given one hundred pounds for her marriage portion and fifty pounds more if she gave up any claim to the cottage in Chapel Lane. If she or any child of hers were living three years after the date of the will, another one hundred and fifty pounds would go to her or her children; so long as she was married she would be paid the interest from this sum but not the principal. Her husband would not receive this one hundred and fifty pounds unless he settled lands of the same value on her and her children. If Judith or a child were not living after three years, one hundred pounds would go to Elizabeth Hall and fifty pounds to Joan Hart or her children. Shakespeare gave Judith his broad silver and gilt bowl. To his sister Joan Hart he gave twenty pounds, all his wearing apparel, and a life-tenancy in the house "wherein she dwelleth" (the western house in Henley Street). He left five pounds apiece to her three sons, remembering the names of William and Michael but not that of Thomas. To his only grandchild Elizabeth Hall he gave all his plate except the bowl given to Judith. From a canceled passage it appears that he had planned to arrange a marriage portion for Elizabeth, but since she was only eight and her mother might have other children he left it to her parents to provide for her. He could count on the Halls to look after Mrs. Shakespeare, but he gave her a special bequest of "my second best bed with the furniture," which may have been the one she preferred.[13]

Shakespeare bequeathed five pounds to Thomas Russell and twenty marks to Francis Collins of Warwick, asking them to serve as overseers of the will. He gave ten pounds to the poor of Stratford, his sword to Thomas Combe, and twenty shillings in gold to his godson William Walker. To buy each a ring to wear in his memory, he left two marks apiece to Hamnet Sadler, William Reynolds, Anthony and John Nash, and "to my ffellowes John Hemynge Richard Burbage & Henry Cundell." He signed his name at the end, "By me William Shakspeare," and he also signed the first and second sheets, with the spelling "Shakspere." Thomas Combe the elder had declared in his will, also witnessed by Collins, "In wittnes that this is my last will and that I would have yt putt into further forme of lawe yf neede bee I have unto everye sheete hereof being five in all putt to my marke," and John Combe had declared that he had "unto every sheet hereof written my name." The witnesses to the publishing or declaration by Shakespeare that this was his will were Francis Collins, July or Julyns Shaw, John Robinson, Hamnet Sadler, and Robert Whattcott. Five witnesses had also been named in the will of Shakespeare's grandfather, Robert Arden. Robinson and Whattcott may have been servants of Shakespeare or of Hall. John Robinson, laborer, had a son christened in 1604/5, another John was born in 1589, and men of this name married at Stratford in 1579 and in 1609 and sued in the court of record in 1591 and for assaults in 1607 and 1613. Whattcott sued in 1587 on a bond and in 1604 for damages for sheep worried and killed by dogs, and in 1613 he appeared at Worcester for Susanna Hall.[14]

Joan Hart was five years younger than Shakespeare and outlived him by thirty years. The only one of Shakespeare's four sisters who survived childhood, she married before 1600 William Hart, hatter. He was sued for debts in 1600 by Richard Collins, Robert Cawdrey, and Arthur Ange and in 1601 by William Wyatt, and was buried on April 17, 1616. Their children were William (1600–

1639, not the William Hart, player, who died at London in 1650), Mary (1603–7), Thomas (1605–61), and Michael (1608–18). The western house in Henley Street was occupied by Joan Hart until she died in 1646 and then by her son Thomas. The churchwardens in 1633 "present Thomas hart and Margrett sambage to proufe there marriage." His son Thomas became owner of both houses by the will of Shakespeare's granddaughter, and they passed to Shakespeare Hart in 1694 and to later Harts until the heirs sold the property in 1806. Shakespeare's last descendant, Elizabeth Hall, married in 1626 Thomas Nash and in 1649 John Bernard, who was knighted in 1661. She died in 1670 at Abington, Northamptonshire.[15]

Shakespeare's godson William Walker was probably the William, son of Henry Walker, alderman, christened on October 16, 1608. William Walker, gentleman, became bailiff in 1649 and died in 1680. Henry Walker, a mercer in High Street, was elected bailiff in 1607, 1624, and 1635. He witnessed a deed by Shakespeare's father in 1597, and John Combe in 1613 left twenty shillings to Mr. Henry Walker. The only payment to players at Stratford between 1597 and 1618 was made in 1608 by order of the bailiff, who until October was Walker. Since Walker named a son Maurice, he may have been the Henry Walker christened at Solihull in 1566/7 and related to the Maurice Walker of Solihull who was an overseer of the will of Oliver Greene, grandfather of Shakespeare's cousin. A Thomas Shaxpere was christened at Solihull in 1551 and a Henry Shaxpere was buried there in 1557.[16]

According to John Ward, who became vicar of Stratford in 1662, "Shakespear Drayton and Ben Jhonson had a merry meeting and it seems drank too hard for Shakespear died of a feavour there contracted." Ward's notes are a mixture of truth and hearsay, for he also wrote that Shakespeare "in his elder days lived at Stratford: and supplied y^e stage with 2 plays every year, and for y^t had an allowance so large, y^t hee spent att y^e Rate of a 1,000 $l.$ a year, as I have heard." Shakespeare wrote about two plays a year, but the amount of his wealth was exaggerated. A note on Shakespeare by

Richard Davies before 1708, that "He dyed a papist," is too late to be worth much as evidence.[17]

Shakespeare died on April 23, 1616, and was buried two days later in the chancel of Stratford church, where his wife was buried beside him in 1623. His monument was carved by Gerard Johnson the younger of Southwark, and Martin Droeshout the younger, born in 1601, engraved his portrait for the First Folio.[18]

NOTES

THESE ABBREVIATIONS ARE USED IN THE NOTES:

Accounts   Accounts of the chamberlains of Stratford, Birthplace
                 Library.
Cal.   James Orchard Halliwell[-Phillipps], *A Descriptive
                 Calendar of the Ancient Manuscripts and Records in
                 the Possession of the Corporation of Stratford-upon-
                 Avon*, 1863.
Chambers   Volume II of Sir Edmund Kerchever Chambers, *Wil-
                 liam Shakespeare: A Study of Facts and Problems*, 2
                 vols., 1930.
Contemps.   Charlotte Carmichael Stopes, *Shakespeare's Warwick-
                 shire Contemporaries*, 1907.
Court   Court of Record declarations and register, Birthplace
                 Library (listed in *Cal.*).
DNB   *Dictionary of National Biography.*
Envir.   C. C. Stopes, *Shakespeare's Environment*, 1914.
Family   C. C. Stopes, *Shakespeare's Family*, 1907.
Fines   Feet of Fines, Public Record Office.
Fripp   Edgar Innes Fripp, *Shakespeare: Man and Artist*, 2
                 vols., 1938.
Gray   Joseph William Gray, *Shakespeare's Marriage*, 1905.
H. P.   J. O. Halliwell-Phillipps, *Outlines of the Life of
                 Shakespeare*, 7th edition, 1887; reprinted 1889, 1890,
                 1898.
H. P. (1848)   J. O. Halliwell[-Phillipps], *A Life of William Shake-
                 speare*, 1848.

Haunts	E. I. Fripp, *Shakespeare's Haunts near Stratford,* 1929.
Ingleby	Clement Mansfield Ingleby, *Shakespeare and the Enclosure of Common Fields at Welcombe,* 1885.
KB	Court of King's Bench, Public Record Office.
Lewis	Benjamin Roland Lewis, *The Shakespeare Documents,* 2 vols., 1941 (unreliable but with good facsimiles).
MA	*Minutes and Accounts of the Corporation of Stratford-upon-Avon,* ed. Richard Savage and Edgar I. Fripp, Vols. I–IV (from 1553 to 1592), Publications of the Dugdale Society, Vols. I, III, V, X, 1921–30.
Malone	*The Plays and Poems of William Shakespeare,* ed. Edmond Malone, 21 vols., 1821.
MD	Miscellaneous Documents, borough records at the Birthplace Library, 16 vols. (listed in *Cal.*).
P.R.O.	Public Record Office, London.
Quyny	E. I. Fripp, *Master Richard Quyny,* 1924.
Rarities	J. O. Halliwell-Phillipps, *A Calendar of the Shakespeare Rarities . . . at Hollingbury Copse,* 2d edition, 1891 (a collection now at the Folger Shakespeare Library, Washington).
Requests	Court of Requests, Public Record Office.
Stratford	E. I. Fripp, *Shakespeare's Stratford,* 1928.
Studies	E. I. Fripp, *Shakespeare Studies,* 1930.
VHW	*The Victoria History of the County of Warwick,* 6 vols. and index vol., 1904–55.
Waters	Henry Fitz-Gilbert Waters, *Genealogical Gleanings in England,* 2 vols., 1901 (wills).
Wellstood	*Catalogue of the Books, Manuscripts, Works of Art, Antiquities and Relics Exhibited in Shakespeare's Birthplace,* ed. Frederick Christian Wellstood, 1925; 1944 edition with supplement.
Wheler MSS	Robert Bell Wheler's collection of records, Birthplace Library (*A Brief Hand-List* was published by Halliwell[-Phillipps], 1863).
Wills	Edgar Vine Hall, *Wills from Shakespeare's Town and Time,* 2 vols., first series, 1931; second series, 1933.

The early registers of Stratford are printed in *The Registers of Stratford-on-Avon*, ed. Richard Savage, 3 vols., Parish Register Society, Vols. VI, XVI, LV, 1897–1905. The history of the town has been written by Philip Styles in *The Victoria History of the County of Warwick*, III (1945), 221–88, and by Levi Fox, *The Borough Town of Stratfordupon-Avon*, 1953. Records of Shakespeare at Stratford are most fully presented by Halliwell-Phillipps. Chambers is valuable for discussion and for further references.

CHAPTER I

1   Sir William Dugdale, *The Antiquities of Warwickshire* (1656); *VHW*, II–IV (1906–47).

2   *The Register of the Guild of Knowle*, ed. W. B. Bickley (1894); Henry Norris in *Notes and Queries*, VIII.viii (1895), 501–2, reprinted in his *Baddesley Clinton* (1897), 122–23; J. P. Yeatman, *The Gentle Shakspere* (1896), 160; Elisabeth G. Kimball in *Times Literary Supplement*, May 9, 1936; C. L. Ewen in *Notes and Queries*, 172 (1937), 259; Rupert Taylor in *PMLA*, LV (1940), 721–26. The P.R.O. reference for the survey of about 1538 is E315/361 (membrane 5).

3   *The Register of the Guild of Knowle*; J. W. Ryland, *Records of Rowington* (2 vols., 1896, 1922) and *Records of Wroxall Abbey and Manor* (1903); Chambers 356–63.

4   Joseph Hunter, *New Illustrations of Shakespeare* (1845), I.8; Chambers 355, 367; C. L. Ewen in *Miscellanea Genealogica et Heraldica*, 5th series, VII (1929–31), 239–41, and *A History of Surnames of the British Isles* (1931), 313; Dugdale Soc. XIX.69.

5   "Richardus Shakyspere in Goodes," subsidy for 14–15 Henry VIII, P.R.O., E179/192/128 (misdated by Yeatman and Chambers); Folger MSS Z.e.7 and Z.e.8, listed in *Rarities*, nos. 217, 246; Folger MS Z.c.36 (18); Warwick Castle MS 2662; Fines, Hilary term, 1 James I; Hunter I.9–13; H. P. II.246–47; George Miller, *The Parishes of the Diocese of Worcester* (1889), I.148; Yeatman 142, 160, 161, 164, 192; Chambers 13–14, 366–67; Leslie Hotson in *The Times*, July 6, 1935, and *Shakespeare's Sonnets Dated* (1949), 218–19, 223; Rupert Taylor in *PMLA*, LX (1945), 90–93.

6   P.R.O., court rolls of Warwick College; Richard Savage, *Shake-
     spearean Extracts from "Edward Pudsey's Booke"* (1888), 81–82;
     Yeatman 172; N. J. Hone, *The Manor and Manorial Records*
     (1906), 125, 308–10; Chambers 26–28.
7   Survey and Trevelyan MSS at Birthplace; H. P. II.207–13; E. I.
     Fripp in *Notes and Queries,* XII.viii (1921), 24–25; *MA* I.112–
     13; Chambers 26–28; Fripp I.35–36.
8   H. P. II.173, 207–8; *Envir.* 12–14, 31–35; Chambers 26–28.
9   H. P. II.179–82, 207; Halliwell-Phillipps, *The Visits of Shake-
     speare's Company* (1887), 44–46; Gray 259–60; *Envir.* 21; Fripp
     in *Notes and Queries,* XII.vii (1920), viii (1921); *Studies* 1–4;
     Fripp I.33–36; Lewis I.19–23.
10   Inventory of John Pardie, Worcestershire Record Office; MD i.89,
     99; H. P. II.209–12, 241–43, 407–8; *Envir.* 63–68.
11   Trevelyan MSS; H. P. II.209–12.
12   H. P. II.209–12, 241–43; *Envir.* 66–71; *Haunts* 100–105; Cham-
     bers 14–16; Fripp I.176–80.
13   Trevelyan MSS; Folger MS 1468.2, quoted in Frank Marcham,
     William Shakespeare and His Daughter Susannah (1931); MD
     i.93, 102, 104, v.30, vii.130, 131; Birthplace Deed 548, printed in
     Savage, *"Edward Pudsey's Booke,"* p. vi; *Cal.* 123, 454–55; H. P.
     II.212–13 (the entry dated 1575 was for 1581); *Haunts* 90–91;
     Chambers 14–17; Wellstood (1944 edn.), no. 26b.
14   Parish registers at Shire Hall, Warwick; will of John Pardie, Wor-
     cestershire Record Office; Yeatman 153, 174; Chambers 3, 13–18;
     Taylor in *PMLA,* LV (1940), 726.
15   Dugdale, 302, 675; G. R. French, *Shakspeareana Genealogica*
     (1869), 431–41; E. A. Freeman, *History of the Norman Conquest*
     (1870–71 edn.), IV.780; *VHW* I.277–78, IV.45, 61–62; J. H.
     Round, *Peerage and Pedigree* (1910), II.127; *The Place-Names of
     Warwickshire,* English Place-Name Soc., XIII (1936), 11–12;
     A. R. Wagner, *English Genealogy* (1960), 47–48.
16   Dugdale, 641–49, 675–81; George Baker, *History of Northampton-
     shire* (1820), I.67, 516; French 446–50; *Close Rolls, 1447–54,*
     198–99; J. C. Wedgwood, *History of Parliament, 1439–1509,* I
     (1936), 18–19; *VHW* IV.45, 62.
17   P.R.O., C1, 275/22, 278/70, and 461/29; Dugdale, 678; Malone

II.36, 544–46; Hunter, II.332; French, 450–55; *Register of the Guild of Knowle*, 20, 207; *Family* 170–73; P.R.O., *Lists and Indexes*, XIII.10, 173, XXIX.111, 121, XXXVIII.211; *Patent Rolls, 1494–1509*, 264, 459, 475, 534; *Letters and Papers of Henry VIII*, I (1920), i.12, 13, 239, 263, IV.i.868, and *Addenda*, I.ii.186.

18 Birthplace manor records; H. P. II.366; *Lists and Indexes*, IX.177; *Family* 188; *The Register of the Gild of Stratford*, ed. J. H. Bloom (1907), 86; Chambers 31–32; Ewen in *Notes and Queries*, 183 (1942), 235; Dugdale Soc. XIX.48; A. B. Emden, *Biographical Register of the University of Oxford*, I (1957).

19 MD ii.4, 83; Dugdale, 560; Halliwell[-Phillipps], *A New Boke about Shakespeare* (1850), 14–16; H. P. II.207; *Family* 27–30, 184; *Envir.* 12–14; *Letters and Papers of Henry VIII*, I.i.221; J. S. Smart, *Shakespeare: Truth and Tradition* (1928), 64; C. W. Throckmorton, *The Throckmorton Family* (1930), 102–4; William Cooper, *The Records of Beaudesert* (1931), 9–10; Mildred Campbell, *The English Yeoman* (1942), 125; Dugdale Soc. XVIII.203; *VHW* III.25, 60; *Close Rolls, 1485–1500*, 112.

20 P.R.O., E179/192/128 and C142/43/50; Hunter, I.33–34; H. P. (1848), 12; H. P. II.367; Yeatman, 172; *Family* 31; *MA* I.105.

21 MD ii.9, 59; Birthplace Deed 428; H. P. II.173; Hone, *The Manor*, 125, 310; *Envir.* 14–16, 34; Dugdale Soc. II.92.

22 Malone II.23–24; Hunter I.37–43; H. P. (1848), 6–8; H. P. II.366–69; *Register of Knowle*, 236; Yeatman, introd. to 3d edn. (1906), 12; *Register of the Gild of Stratford*, 219; Chambers 30–31; *VHW* III.44.

23 H. P. II.199–201, 371; Oliver Baker, *In Shakespeare's Warwickshire* (1937), 223–60; *VHW* III.38.

24 MD ii.21 (endorsed as the copy given to "Johan Lambert"), 73 ("Alice Ardern"), 77 ("Margaret Webbe"), 79 ("Kateryn Edkyns"), all dated July 17, 4 Edward VI; H. P. II.173–76; *Envir.* 17.

25 Malone II.538–41; H. P. II.53–54; Henry Gee, *The Elizabethan Clergy* (1898), 183, 253, 286; Gray 261–63; Fripp in *Notes and Queries*, XII.viii (1921), 124–25; Taylor in *PMLA*, LX (1945), 91.

26 MD i.88, ii.13; H. P. II.54–55, 177–78, 371–72.

27 Bearley register at Shire Hall, Warwick; Trevelyan MSS; MD i.92,
    ii.10, 15, 20, 78, vii.41; *Envir.* 19–23.
28 MD ii.12, 80, 84, vii.153; H. P. II.11–13, 54, 175, 370; *Envir.*
    26–27, 33.
29 MD ii.10, 20; Warwick Castle MS 2646; H. P. II.55; *Envir.* 21–
    22; *Haunts* 58.
30 Birthplace Deed 433; MD ii.74; Warwick Castle MS 2646;
    Hunter I.37; *Envir.* 29–31; *Haunts* 58.
31 Birthplace Deed 429; H. P. II.177–78, 407–8; *Envir.* 19, 34; *MA*
    I.94; *Haunts* 93.
32 Trevelyan MSS; Snitterfield register at Shire Hall, Warwick; MD
    ii.7, 10; Birthplace Deeds 429–32; H. P. II.235; *Envir.* 18–35.
33 Trevelyan MSS; Snitterfield register; MD ii.14; *Envir.* 21–35;
    Haunts 97–99.

CHAPTER II

1   MD xi.7; *MA* I.xxxii–iv; *Haunts* 88–91; *VHW* III.240, 242.
2   H. P. II.215–16; *MA* I.xx, 57–58, IV.96; Dugdale Soc. XVIII.
    216–17.
3   Hunter, *New Illustrations of Shakespeare,* I.31; H. P. I.26, II.
    215–46; *Worcester Wills,* British Record Soc. XXXI, 161; *Family*
    119; *MA* I.xxxiv–vi.
4   H. P. I.40, II.216–25; *MA* I.xxxvi, 90, 93, 101, 119, 134; *Strat-
    ford* 24–26; C. J. Sisson in *The Library,* IV.ix (1928), 22; Fripp
    I.34–37.
5   H. P. II.219–27; *MA* I.xlix–lvi, 120–52.
6   Malone II.64; *MA* I.lii, lx, III.42.
7   Malone II.94–95; Alfred Beesley, *The History of Banbury* (1841),
    220; H. P. II.227–32; *MA* I.145–47, II.xv–xxxiv, 5–71; Hotson,
    Shakespeare versus Shallow (1931), 38; Fripp I.42–44, 71; Well-
    stood (1944 edn.), no. 25a.
8   H. P. I.383–84; *V. H. Worcs.* IV.357; Hotson in *The Times,* Dec.
    29, 1926, and *Shakespeare's Sonnets Dated,* 233–38; *MA* IV.57–
    60; Chambers 5, 33; Lewis I.112–13.
9   H. P. II.233–41; *MA* II.112, III.11–31, 168–70; Chambers, *Wil-
    liam Shakespeare,* I.14–15, II.20. The September entry suggests
    that an error was made in marking him present on August 31,
    1586.

10 Fines, 21 and 44 Eliz.; H. P. II.11–17, 202–5, 235–36, 367–71; *Envir.* 41–47; Chambers 35–39.

11 H. P. II.53, 199–205; Chambers 38–39.

12 Fines, 21 and 22 Eliz.; H. P. (1848), 54–59; H. P. II.176–82; *Envir.* 23–25; Wellstood, no. 27; Chambers 40.

13 P.R.O., KB27/1274 and E101/109/13, mems. 20d, 21; *Envir.* 41–42; *MA* III.xxxvi–xl, 68–69; Fripp I.160–66.

14 MD vii.139; Court; *Cal.* 197, 460, 461; H. P. II.245; *MA* I.94, 104, III.91, 100, IV.21; Hotson in *The Times,* Oct. 1, 1931, and *Shakespeare's Sonnets Dated,* 224–29.

15 Malone II.51–62; H. P. II.137–40, 238–40, 243–46; *MA* III.155, IV.21, 148; Chambers 3; Taylor in *PMLA,* LV (1940), 721.

16 MD i.3, vii.142; H. P. II.238–45; *MA* IV.1–2, 154–57.

17 Court; P.R.O., C24/222/4; Warwick Castle MS 2662; Accounts; H. P. (1848), 126; *Cal.* 173, 197–201, 456–64; *The Seconde Parte of a Register,* ed. Peel (1915), II.107; *MA* IV.xxxiv–xl, 148–51, 159–62; Chambers, *William Shakespeare,* I.15; Hotson, *Shakespeare's Sonnets Dated,* 233–38.

18 MD vi.168, 176; *Cal.* 160, 172; *Envir.* 72–73; *MA* III.107.

19 MD vi.170, vii.244–46; Council Book B, 178; Halliwell[-Phillipps], *A New Boke about Shakespeare* (1850), 48–51; *The Works of William Shakespeare,* ed. Halliwell[-Phillipps], I (1853), 139–40; *Cal.* 344–45, 361; *Envir.* 61–62; *Quyny* 92–95.

20 J. P. Collier in *Archaeologia,* XXXV (1853), 20–22; *The Works of William Shakespeare,* ed. Halliwell[-Phillipps], I (1853), 33–35; H. P. I.390–92; Wellstood, no. 28; *Stratford* 19–20.

21 Hotson in *The Times,* Nov. 22, 1930, and *Shakespeare's Sonnets Dated,* 231–33. Another glover, John Lock, sold a tod of "fell wooll" in 1558: *Cal.* 184.

22 MD v.20; H.P. II.248; *Quyny* 177.

23 Chambers 247.

24 Wills and inventories in MD and Wheler MSS; *Cal.* 64–66; *VHW* III.280. A spiritual testament attributed to one "John Shakspear" has not been shown to have had any connection with Shakespeare's father. John Jordan, who was born in 1746, claimed that the MS had been found by a bricklayer in 1757 between the rafters and the tiling of the Birthplace, but there is no proof of his story. Malone in 1790 described the MS, which is now lost, as containing five

leaves; when he inquired for the missing first leaf, Jordan pretended that he had seen it and sent Malone a faked copy. The five leaves were an English translation of a spiritual testament composed by St. Charles Borromeo (d. 1584), probably distributed by Jesuit missionaries in 1580 and later, since William Allen wrote in 1581 that Father Parsons "wants three or four thousand or more of the Testaments." Blank spaces were left in these copies to be filled in with the names of the testator and of his patron saint; in the lost MS the names were "John Shakespear" and "saint Winefride." There were, of course, many John Shakespeares, and Jordan is known to have practised forging the signature of William Shakespeare. See Malone, *The Plays and Poems of William Shakspeare* (1790), I.ii.161 ff., 330 ff., and *An Inquiry* (1796), 198–99; R. B. Wheler, *A Guide to Stratford-upon-Avon* (1814), 143; H. P. II. 399–404; Chambers 380–82; and J. H. de Groot, *The Shakespeares and "the Old Faith"* (1946), 64–110, a more careful study of the evidence for the document than that in Heinrich Mutschmann and Karl Wentersdorf, *Shakespeare and Catholicism* (1953).

CHAPTER III

1 *Studies* 13–44.
2 H. P. I.377–85; Chambers 32–34.
3 MD v.6, 44; *Cal.* 131, 189; Halliwell[-Phillipps], *Abstracts and Copies of Indentures Respecting Estates in Henley Street* (1866); H. P. I.377–79, II.216, 232–33; *The Black Book of Warwick,* ed. Thomas Kemp (1898), 208; *MA* I.ix, 104, 113, 116, II.xliii, 33, 84, III.80; Wellstood, nos. 25, 26; *Stratford* 15–16.
4 MD vii.61; *MA* I.113, IV.12, 28–29, 34; *Stratford* 15, 22–23; Fripp II. 528–29.
5 MD vii.142, 149; *MA* I.113, 133–34, II.15, 84, 107–9, III. lvii–lx, 34, 170, IV.29, 37, 58, 96, 149, 154–55, 161; *Haunts* 46–50.
6 MD i.16, vii.31; Court; Malone II.71–72, 546; *MA* II.85, III.16, 108, 156–57, IV.89, 155–57; *Stratford* 3–7, 13; *Wills* I.16–18, II.22–25; Hotson, *Shakespeare's Sonnets Dated,* 224–29.
7 *MA* I.51, II.105, 113, III.18, 97, 135, 138, IV.155–57; *Quyny* 19, 28.

8 MD iii.41, vii.150; *MA* II.85, III.37, 152, 158, IV.30; Fripp I.182.

9 MD v.9; H. P. II.242; *MA* II.5–8, 27–28, 83–84; *Quyny* 25–27, 39–41, 87–88, 163; *Stratford* 70–71; *Wills* II.36–40; *VHW* III. 230.

10 *MA* II.5, 28–42, III.29, IV.60–63; *Stratford* 3, 39–40; Fripp I. 136–37; *VHW* III.229–30.

11 Birthplace wills, no. 30; MD i.7; *MA* I.77, 84, II.83, III.107, 126, IV.79, 81, 103.

12 *MA* I.47, 60, III.48, 140, 159, IV.103.

13 Malone II.56–57; *MA* II.83, III.72, 107.

14 *Register of the Guild of Knowle,* 84; *MA* II.82, 118, III.10, 13, 45, 105, 149; *Quyny* 13 ff.; *Stratford* 33–34.

15 *MA* II.36, 82, III.15, 26; *Quyny* 172, 177; *Studies* 26–29, 55–61, 76–77.

16 Warwick Castle MSS 2648, 2663; *Studies* 69–75, 79; *VHW* III. 225–26.

17 *MA* II.82; *Stratford* 13; *Wills* II.10–14.

18 MD i.14, 25, iii.34, 39, vi.68; *Cal.* 180, 185, 187, 191, 449; *Quyny* 22–25.

19 *Cal.* 462; *MA* I.120, 126, 134, II.33, 81–82; *Quyny* 27–29, 81, 107, 113–16, 122, 163–64; *Stratford* 37–39; Fripp II.576; *VHW* III.239.

20 *MA* II.81; *Stratford* 41–42; Fripp I.89; *VHW* III.227.

21 *Cal.* 136–37; *MA* II.8, 80, III.105; *Stratford* 51–55; *Studies* 62–64; *VHW* III.228.

22 *Contemps.* 216–18; *MA* III.77, IV.110; *Haunts* 127–28, 137–38; Chambers 97, 127–32; *VHW* III.262, 275–76.

23 Folger MS 1468.2, quoted in Frank Marcham, *William Shakespeare and His Daughter Susannah* (1931) ; *Collectanea Topographica et Genealogica,* VIII (1843), 301–8; *MA* III.57–58, IV.42–44.

24 P.R.O., C24/191/36, depositions for Lodowick Greville; Chancery Miscellanea, 82/9/267, certiorari and verdict at Warwick assizes; Harleian Soc. XII.306–7; *Notes and Queries,* XII.vii (1920), 382; *Quyny* 188; *Stratford* 30–31; *Haunts* 63, 148–54; Chambers 13; *VHW* III.285–87.

25 Council Book B, 38, 114; MD i.110, v.218–20, xvi.13; Accounts; Fines, Hilary, 3 Jas.; H. P. (1848), 105; *DNB* under Byfield;

Parish Register Soc. VI; Waters I.114–15, II.1389–95; J. H. Bloom, *Shakespeare's Church* (1902), 144; *Contemps.* 234–36; *MA* III.136, IV.xvi, xxx, 3, 7, 121–23, 127, 145, 148, 152; *Stratford* 55–56, 70–71; *Haunts* 74–75; *Studies* 13–49; *Wills* II.36–40.
26 Accounts; MD xii.64; *Cal.* 417; H. P. II.196; *MA* I.121–51, II. 35–99, III.13, 95, 117; *Quyny* 60–61; *Studies* 74, 79; William Cooper, *Wootton Wawen* (1936), 77; Fripp I.361.

CHAPTER IV

1 MD xii.40; Accounts; *VHW* II.334–38; *MA* I.19–21, 35–36, 121–22, 128, 140, 151; Hugh Savage, *Annals of Shakespeare's School* (1911), typescript at Birthplace, copy at Folger; *Quyny* 60–61, 120–21, 166–67, 203; *Studies* 74; T. W. Baldwin, *William Shakspere's Small Latine & Lesse Greeke* (1944), I.464–69.
2 *Studies* 20–25, 31–51; Baldwin, I.567.
3 *Cal.* 142, where 1604 should read 1582; *MA* II.xxiii, 81, III.106; *Quyny* 40; Wellstood, nos. 25, 26; Fripp I.89; Baldwin, I.467–68. "Gualterus Roche" signed six deeds now at the Birthplace and one in Folger MS Z.c.36 (136).
4 Gray 108–9; J. H. Pollen in *The Month*, Oct.-Nov., 1917; Fripp I.89–91; Baldwin, I.468–77.
5 *MA* II.xl–xli, III.45; Fripp I.91–92; Baldwin, I.468–82.
6 Catholic Record Soc. V.18–19; *MA* III.33, 38–39, 48, 117; Baldwin, I.480–88; Robert Stevenson, *Shakespeare's Religious Frontier* (1958), 64–70.
7 MD. iii.8, lease printed in H. P. (1848), 94–95; KB29/228; Council Book B; Warwick Castle MS 2663; Fane MS, printed by E. M. Martin in *English Review*, LI (1930), 484–89; *The Spending of the Money of Robert Nowell*, ed. Grosart (1877), 238–39; *VHW* II.337; *The Genealogist*, new series, XXXIII (1917), 166; *Quyny* 33, 61–64, 120–21; *MA* III.117–64, IV.154–55; *Stratford* 48–51; *Studies* 75–81; Fripp I.401–3, II.497, 642–46, 702, 800; Baldwin, I.466–89.
8 Harleian MS 1471, f. 98; Hunter, *New Illustrations of Shakespeare*, I.47; Waters I.612; T. F. Kirby, *Winchester Scholars* (1888), 149; *Studies* 22, 27, 59–60; Hotson, *Shakespeare's Sonnets Dated*, 131–32.

9 Corporation of London Records, Orphans Ledger I.79, 80; Arber, *Transcript of the Stationers' Register; Contemps.* 1–22; A. E. M. Kirwood in *The Library*, IV.xii (1931), 1–39.

10 P.R.O., Requests 2/416/90, 2/435; MD i.21, vi.65; *Cal.* 160, 172; Waters I.621; *Stratford* 51–54; *Studies* 62–66.

11 *Diaries of the English College, Douay*, ed. T. F. Knox (1878), 194–221; Gianluigi Andrich, *De Natione Anglica et Scota Iuristarum Universitatis Patavinae* (1892), 133 ff.; Catholic Record Soc. XVIII.346; *MA* III.9–10, IV.148, 160, 162.

12 Council Book B; *Cal.* 119, 123, 154; Ingleby 3, 4, 6, 11.

13 Folger MS Z.e.9; Harleian Soc. XII.307; Ingleby 8; Waters I.619–20; *Haunts* 148–50.

14 Chambers 252–53.

CHAPTER V

1 *VHW* III.233.

2 H. P. II.184–85, 195–96; *MA* III.87.

3 Gray, with facsimiles; Chambers 41–46.

4 Bonds in MD xiii.62, 77; Gray; Chambers 43–45.

5 Clarence Hopper, *Churchwardens' Presentments* (1867), 16–17; H. P. I.64; Gray 65–69, 190–96, 205, 225; *MA* III.lv.

6 MD vii.147, John Haines; H. P. II.364; Gray 16, 36–47; *MA* IV.5; Chambers 46–47.

7 H. P. II.190–96, 362; *Haunts* 4–6; Chambers 47–49.

8 MD i.11; H. P. (1848), 116–19; H. P. II.187, 195–96, 225–30; *MA* II.1–2, III.86–90; *Haunts* 6–10, 27–28, 44–45; *Wills* II. 10–17; Lewis I.155–57.

9 P.R.O., C24/170, depositions for Francis Smith, esquire, defendant to Ambrose, Earl of Warwick; C. J. Sisson in *Shakespeare Survey 12* (1959), 95–106.

10 Warwick Castle MSS 2653, 2657; *Archaeologia*, XXXII (1847), 444–45; H. P. II.190, 364; Gray 28–29, 223; *MA* IV.112; *Haunts* 9–10; Chambers 42–43. Another shepherd, Richard Cowper, left most of his money as "due dett in the handes of Abraham Sturley" (*Quyny* 51).

11 KB27/1395; *Cal.* 464; H. P. II.186–98; *Haunts* 11–15.

12 Fripp I.192–94, 198.

CHAPTER VI

1 *Annalia Dubrensia,* ed. Grosart (1877), 43–44; Chambers 247.

2 Chambers, *William Shakespeare,* I.17, II.252–54; G. E. Bentley, *The Jacobean and Caroline Stage,* II (1941), 363–74; Baldwin, *William Shakspere's Small Latine & Lesse Greeke,* I.34–38.

3 Chambers 259; Baldwin, I.45–51.

4 Chambers, *William Shakespeare,* I.18–21, II.257, 265, 279–80, 289–90.

5 *The Autobiography and Personal Diary of Dr. Simon Forman,* ed. Halliwell (1849), 11; *DNB; Quyny* 39, 92, 120–21; Eccles in *Thomas Lodge and Other Elizabethans,* ed. Sisson (1933), 420; W. H. Challen in *Notes and Queries,* 202 (1957), 290–92, 324–26.

6 Chetham Soc. LI (1860), 237–41; Oliver Baker, *In Shakespeare's Warwickshire and the Unknown Years* (1937), 297–319; Chambers, *Shakespearean Gleanings* (1944), 52–56; Alan Keen and Roger Lubbock, *The Annotator* (1954), 34–35, 75–81, and Keen in *Times Literary Supplement,* April 21, 1950, and Nov. 18, 1955, and in *Bulletin of the John Rylands Library,* XXXIII (1950–51), 256–70; Robert Stevenson, *Shakespeare's Religious Frontier* (1958), 67–83.

7 Lucy MSS at Shire Hall, Warwick; Malone II.123–32, 356–57; John Nichols, *The Progresses of Queen Elizabeth* (1823), I.295, 320; Alfred Beesley, *The History of Banbury* (1841), 226; H. P. II.386–89; Alexander Brown, *The Genesis of the United States* (1890), II.992 (from the Sandys family Bible at Hawkshead school); *DNB; Contemps.* 23–41; J. T. Murray, *English Dramatic Companies* (1910), II.88, 238; *MA* II.xxx, xxxii, III.97; *Quyny* 38–39; *Stratford* 11–12; *Haunts* 113–22; Alice Fairfax-Lucy, *Charlecote and the Lucys* (1958), 66–97.

8 Accounts for 1604; MD xiii.96; H. P. (1848), 103; *DNB;* Gray 10; *Contemps.* 42–54; *Haunts* 122–25; Bentley, II.484, 618; Mary F. Keeler, *The Long Parliament* (1954), 259–60; Alice Fairfax-Lucy, 99–140.

9 Accounts for 1605; Joseph Edmondson, *The Family of Greville* (1766), 74–75; Camden, *Britannia* (1806 edn.), II.445; H. P. II. 388–89; *Hatfield MSS,* XI.433–34; *Contemps.* 164–65; *MA* III.

5, 65, 97, 135, 149, IV.17, 32, 42, 55–56, 73, 145, 162–63; Fripp I.
151, 160, 218–21, II.548–49, 642, 645; *VHW* III.250.

10 KB29/226, membranes 33, 34, 37d; Dugdale, *Warwickshire*
(1656), 534–35; *Acts of the Privy Council, 1588–1590; Contemps.*
162–64; *MA* III.80, 136, IV.42; *VHW* V.200.

11 MD ix.14; Wheler MSS i.89; Dugdale, 535; *Collectanea Topo-graphica et Genealogica,* VIII (1843), 205; H. P. (1848), 101–
4; *Cal. S. P. Dom. 1595–97,* 231, and *1598–1601,* 226; *Commons
Papers, 1878,* LXII.i.430, 446; W. A. Shaw, *The Knights of England* (1896), II.94 ("Lodowick" is an error for "Edward"); *Hatfield MSS,* X.107; *Quyny* 83–201; *MA* IV.118–19, 162–63;
Haunts 152–53; Chambers 148; *Sackville MSS; VHW* III.259,
V.200.

12 P.R.O., C24/170; *Camden Miscellany,* IX.iii.7; *Contemps.* 30;
MA III.65, 148, IV.113; English Place-Name Soc. XIII.241; William Cooper, *Wootton Wawen* (1936), 21–24, 112–13; *VHW* III.
198, 205, 225, 260; C. J. Sisson in *Shakespeare Survey 12* (1959),
95–106.

13 P.R.O., E372/434, Warwicks; Baga de Secretis in *Deputy Keeper's
Reports,* IV.232–33; *DNB; Contemps.* 68–108; *Quyny* 45–46;
MA III.64.

14 Dugdale, 586; *MA* III.54, 80, IV.110; Hotson, *I, William Shakespeare* (1937), 171–202; *VHW* III.261, V.111–12, 311.

15 Nichols, *Progresses of Queen Elizabeth,* I.310–16; *DNB;* Venn,
Alumni Cantabrigienses; MA III.5, 13, 15, 67, 96, 118, 134, 150,
IV.17; *Patent Rolls, 1553,* 235-39.

16 *MA* III.118–19, 135, 137, 147, 149, IV.17, 31.

17 Malone II.149–50; *MA* II.xxxiv, 35; Fripp I.61–64.

18 Chambers, *The Elizabethan Stage,* II.86–89, 97–98; *MA* II.77,
105–6, III.13–14.

19 J. T. Murray, *English Dramatic Companies* (1910); Chambers,
The Elizabethan Stage, II.104, 221–24; *MA* III.43, 46, 83, 98,
119, 136–37, 148–49, IV.xx, 16.

20 Chambers, *The Elizabethan Stage,* II.104–9; *MA* IV.xx–xxii, 31–
32.

21 P.R.O., Patent Roll, 29 Eliz., part 16 (C66/1301, m. 20); Malone
II.166–67; Chambers, *The Elizabethan Stage,* II.320–21, 327–28;

A. W. Pollard in Peter Alexander, *Shakespeare's Henry VI and Richard III* (1929), 13–21.

22 *Two Gentlemen of Verona,* IV.iv.165–66; *MA* III.129, 137, 143.

CHAPTER VII

1 Malone II.28–41, 88–93, 541–54; Stephen I. Tucker, *The Assignment of Arms to Shakespeare and Arden, 1596–99* (1884), reprinted in *Miscellanea Genealogica et Heraldica,* 2d series, I (1886), 109; H. P. II.56; Chambers 18–26; Lewis I.208–17. The first draft has been followed where the second draft is imperfect.

2 H. P. II.109; Chambers 11–12, 18–25, 182.

3 Malone II.542–44; Tucker; H. P. II.60–61; Chambers 20–32; Lewis I.299–306.

4 Malone II.89–91; H. P. (1848), 178; Tucker; *Quyny* 6, 210; Chambers 22–25; Lewis II.336–46.

5 Folger MS Z.c.36 (98); Halliwell[-Phillipps], *An Historical Account of the New Place, Stratford-upon-Avon* (1864); H. P. II.101–35, 373–74; *Stratford* 42–44; *Haunts* 127–28; *Studies* 7–13; Chambers 95–99; Lewis I.233–36.

6 Folger MSS Z.c.36 (100, 101); P.R.O., C3/34/8, Chancery bill, answer, and replication; Star Chamber 5, B87/5; *Cal. S.P.D. 1547–80,* 235, 309, 415–16, 429, *1566–79,* 353; *New Place,* 12–13; *Contemps.* 216, 228; Lewis I.235–36.

7 *MD* v.15, 68, 69, 184, 186; P.R.O., Star Chamber 5, H9/22; J. C. M. Bellew, *Shakespeare's Home at New Place* (1863), 341–44; *Contemps.* 228; *Studies* 11–12, 53.

8 Folger MS Z.c.36 (103); *MD* ii.1; H. P. (1848), 101, 165–66; H. P., *New Place,* 15–19; Harleian Soc. XII.31; H. P. II.104–7; W. Underhill in *Notes and Queries,* VIII.v (1894), 478; *Contemps.* 226–33; *MA* I.lvii-lx, 144–45, II.11-33, IV.56, 159; *Quyny* 110, 165; Chambers 95–98; J. H. Morrison, *The Underhills of Warwickshire* (1932), 146–68; Fripp I.461–64; *VHW* V.95–96. Both exemplifications of the 1602 fine were preserved by Sir John Clopton of New Place, by the Ingrams of Wolford, and by their heirs the Severnes of Shropshire, and are now Folger MSS Z.c.36 (110, 111).

9 H. P. II.373–74.

10 Folger MS S.a.115, printed in H. P., *New Place*, 181–222; H. P. II.101–35, 373–79.

11 Folger MS Z.c.36 (100); H. P., *New Place*, 13–236; H. P., *Illustrations of the Life of Shakespeare*, Part I (1874), 65–79; H. P. II.103–27, 378.

12 Stowe MSS at the Huntington Library; H. P. II.99; *Huntington Library Bulletin*, no. 1 (1931), 199–201; E. F. Gay in *Huntington Library Quarterly*, I (1938), II (1939); Lewis II.585–86.

13 Harrison, *Description of England* (1577), Book II, Chap. 6; MD i.106, iii.23, iv.63, v.103, xii.75, 95, xvi.37; H. P. (1848), 167–71; *Cal.* 209, 213, 225, 237; *Stratford* 36–37; Chambers 99–101, 113–18; Fripp II.620, 792–93.

14 H. P., *New Place*, 40–43; H. P. II.19, 355–56; Stopes, *Shakespeare's Industry* (1916), 267–69; Chambers 111–13.

15 MD i.135; H. P. II.57–58; Chambers 101–6.

16 *Quyny* 16–17, 47, 59, 83–187; *VHW* III.249.

17 Malone II.485; *Quyny* 137–39; Chambers 102; Lewis I.226–29.

18 MD vii.138; Birthplace wills, no. 38; Harleian Soc. XII.29, 139–40, XXI.238–41, XXVII.27–29; Bristol and Gloucs. Archaeological Soc. IV.222–29, LXXV.105–15, 145; *DNB;* Aubrey, "*Brief Lives,*" ed. Clark (1898), I.130–35; *MA* IV.118; J. W. Gough, *The Superlative Prodigall* (1932); Hotson, *I, William Shakespeare*, 141–47, 201.

19 P.R.O., C24/271/32, deposition by Sir Edward Greville, aged 34 in 1599; *Quyny* 83–121.

20 MD i.135, 136; Malone II.566–72; H. P. II.57–60; *Hatfield MSS* XIII.582–84; *Quyny* 123–48; *MA* IV.115–19; Chambers 103.

21 MD. i.131; H. P. II.58–59; *Quyny* 144–46; Chambers 102–3.

22 MD i.115, 124, 126, 128 (the letter of Oct. 26), 145, v.149; *Quyny* 133–60; Fripp II.497–98.

23 MD i.137, v.17, 19, 150, vii.116, 117, xii.40; Wheler MSS i.44, 48; *Quyny* 157–60; Fripp II.500–502.

24 MD i.138, 143, v.20, 148, 216, ix.18, x.3; Wheler MSS i.50; *Quyny* 164–87.

25 MD i.119, 122, 123, vii.30, xii.60; Accounts; Wheler MSS i.50; *Quyny* 167–96; Fripp II.542–49, 576–78.

26 Waters I.197–98, 621; *Quyny* 199–210; Chambers 104.

27 MD i.106, 112, xii.54; Warwick Castle MSS 2648, 2663; Ac-

counts; Malone II.561–72; *Envir.* 57; *Quyny* 37 ff.; Fripp I.71–72, 122, II.491–500, 545, 702, 786; *VHW* III.230, 249; Alice Fairfax-Lucy, *Charlecote and the Lucys,* 85.

28   H. P. II.17–19, 25, 331; Chambers 107–11; *Warwick County Records,* I.204; Lewis II.329–36; *VHW* III.261.

29   Patent Rolls, 36 Eliz.; Council Book B, 38, 156; H. P. (1848), 103; R. G. Usher, *The Rise and Fall of the High Commission* (1913), 348; Wellstood, no. 75; Chambers 127–34; Fripp I.243, II.706, 732–35.

30   Warwick Castle MSS 2637, 2663; Fines, Hilary, 39 Eliz.; Accounts; MD i.76, 108, iii.23, iv.21, 190, v.174, vii.143, xii.71, 75, 93, xiii.15, 26, 30, xvi.37, 70; Birthplace wills, no. 37; Wheler MSS i.57; Halliwell[-Phillipps], *Collectanea Respecting the Birth-Place* (1865), 19–21; Ingleby 8–11; H. P. I.381–83; *Vestry Minute-Book,* 8; *Envir.* 339; *MA* IV.111; Chambers 110–11, 149.

31   Bearley register at Shire Hall, Warwick; MD vii.146, 148; inventory at Birthplace; *Cal.* 467; *Envir.* 57–60; *Haunts* 51–52; Fripp I.119–24; *VHW* III.379.

32   MD ii.2, 3, vii.125, x.23; H. P. (1848), 103, 105, 209–17, 299–309; H. P. II.19–31, 348–49; Chambers 118–27; Lewis II.373–85.

33   MD vi.71, vii.116; Dugdale, 552–53; H. P. (1848), 101; *MA* III.17, 59, 124, 137, IV.55, 126, 144; E. A. B. Barnard, *New Links with Shakespeare* (1930), 60–61; *VHW* III.124–26.

34   MD ii.11, vii.125–29, x.8, 9, 10, 23, xii.113, xvi.59; H. P. II.25–31; *V. H. Berks* III.249; Chambers 122–27; *VHW* III.279–80.

35   Fines, 26 Eliz.; Court; MD vi.137; Council Book B, 253; Dugdale, 577 (misnumbered 557); H. P. II.78–80; Wellstood, nos. 49–55; Chambers 114–18; *VHW* V.174.

36   H. P. II.51–52, 343; Chambers 2, 7, 18; Fripp II. 686–87.

37   H. P. II.298–99; *The Churchwardens' Accounts of St. Nicholas, Warwick,* ed. Richard Savage (1890), 84, 86; *Envir.* 332–35; Wellstood, no. 58; Chambers 2, 7; Hotson, *Shakespeare's Sonnets Dated,* 230–31.

38   P.R.O., order in Requests 2/431, affidavits in Requests 1/28.

39   MD i.65, iii.23; *Cal.* 207; *Quyny* 152; *MA* IV.149, 162.

40   MD i.128, vii.69; Fines, Michaelmas, 3 Jas.; KB27/1408, m. 519; Harleian Soc. XXIX.362.

41 MD i.76, 120, 148, iii.15, v.20, vii.2, 10, 20, 23, 143, viii.2, xiii.5; Council Book B, 178; Ingleby 11–12; Wellstood, no. 59; *Wills* II.41–43; Fripp II.548.

CHAPTER VIII

1 Venn, *Alumni Cantabrigienses,* II (1922), 286; Frank Marcham, *William Shakespeare and His Daughter Susannah* (1931); Irvine Gray in *The Genealogists' Magazine,* VII (1936–37), 344–54, 478–79.

2 Accounts, 1611 for Sturley, 1612 and later for Hall; R. B. Wheler, *A Guide to Stratford-upon-Avon* (1814), 26-40; H. P. II.320–21.

3 Council Book B; Fines, Easter, 3 Jas., Ralph Smith; MD xii.93; Consistory Court records in Worcester Diocesan Registry; Harleian MS 4064, f. 189; *Cal.* 226; Clarence Hopper, *Churchwardens' Presentments* (1867), 12; H. P. I.242-44, 394; Waters I.615; *Haunts* 150–54; Chambers 12–13; *Wills* II.41–42; C. J. Sisson, *Lost Plays of Shakespeare's Age* (1935), 190; Fripp II.645, 813, 841–42, 873.

4 MD viii.1, 303; H. P., *New Place,* 92–108; H. P. I.247, 271, II.61, 99, 322–23; *Vestry Minute-Book,* 34–36, 42; *Contemps.* 173–84; *Alumni Cantabrigienses; Studies* 168–71; Marcham; Fripp II.833, 881–92, 902.

5 Folger MS X.d.164 (3); Wheler MSS i.94; Hall, *Select Observations* (1657); J. H. Fennell, *The Shakespeare Repository* (1853), 9–12; H. P., *New Place,* 93–108; Chambers 11–12; Fripp II.881–83; C. M. Mitchell, *The Shakespeare Circle, A Life of Dr. John Hall* (1947), 74–86, 112.

6 Wheler MSS i.58; Council Book B; MD i.1, 2, 164, vii.120–29, xii.103, xiii.43, xvi.14; H. P. (1848), 234–40; Ingleby 10–12; *Contemps.* 187–209; B. H. Newdigate, *Michael Drayton and His Circle* (1941), 41–55, 187.

7 Throckmorton MSS at Birthplace; P.R.O., C3/376/14, *Thomas Russell* v. *Alice and Thomas Nashe of Rushock;* Valentine Green, *History of the City of Worcester* (1796), II, Appendix, p. xvi; Malone, *Correspondence with the Rev. James Davenport* (1864), 74; Hotson, *I, William Shakespeare, Do Appoint Thomas Russell, Esquire . . .* (1937).

8   Court; MD vi.99, xii.63; Folger MSS 450.1 and Z.e.7, listed in
    Rarities, nos. 141, 214; KB29/248, m. 89d; Council Book B;
    P.R.O., E137/46/3, Estreats, King's Remembrancer, Warwick,
    1614; Wheler MSS i.79–81; Prerogative Court of Canterbury,
    101 Weldon; H. P. (1848), 105, 234–40; H. P. II.24–25, 391;
    F. C. Wellstood, *Records of the Manor of Henley-in-Arden*
    (1919), xx, 84; Wellstood, no. 59; *Wills* I.19–20.

9   H. P. (1848), 234–40; H. P. II.204; Yeatman, *The Gentle Shak-*
    spere, 237; Waters II.1248–50; *MA* IV.35; Chambers 127–38,
    172; *Wills* II.28–31; Hotson, *I, William Shakespeare*, 185; Fripp
    II.803–4.

10   Fane MS, printed by E. M. Martin in *English Review*, LI (1930),
    484–89; Folger MSS 267.2 and 452.5, listed in *Rarities*, no. 754;
    Chambers 138–41, 243, 246, 251–53.

11   H. P. (1848), 104; *Cal.* 77, 93, 355; Ingleby; *Vestry Minute-*
    Book, 20, 32, 33, 38; J. H. Bloom, *Shakespeare's Church* (1902),
    204; Connecticut Historical Soc., XXI (1924), xx, 9, 17, 102, 121;
    Chambers 134–38; *Warwick County Records*, II.xxviii; Hotson,
    I, William Shakespeare, 255–57; *VHW* III.264.

12   Hopper, *Churchwardens' Presentments*, 14, 19; Ingleby 9, 13;
    Vestry Minute-Book, 20, 33, 38, 43; Waters II.1247–48; Chambers
    136–38; Fripp II.873, 899, 907; *VHW* III.264, 282.

13   Fines, Hilary, 1588, and Michaelmas, 1593; P.R.O., Requests
    2/313, 2/393/89; MD viii.175, ix.9, 15, x.22; *Cal.* 464; Harleian
    Soc. XII.147; H. P. II.324; Waters I.618; *Contemps.* 85–86;
    Stratford 9; Barnard, *New Links with Shakespeare*, 115–17, 120;
    Chambers 9–10, 109, 122–26, 142, 172; Fripp II.811.

14   KB29/224, m. 78d; KB29/225, Controlment Roll; MD xii.71,
    83, 102; Accounts; P.R.O., Star Chamber 8/26/10; H. P. (1848),
    105; Harleian Soc. XII.147; Sisson, *Lost Plays*, 188–96; Fripp
    II.839–42.

15   MD vii.10, 23, 99, xii.72; P.R.O., Star Chamber 8/26/10; Tread-
    way Nash, *History of Worcestershire* (1781–82), II.105; H. P.
    (1848), 234–40; *Cal.* 464; Harleian Soc. XII.242–43; *Stratford*
    31, 41–42; *MA* IV.101–14, 149, 162; Chambers 137, 147, 172;
    Wills I.21–22; Fripp II. 795–97, 803, 839–42.

16   Warwick Castle MS 2663; MD i.106, 164, v.151, vii.66, 106,
    viii.1, xii.93, xvi.14; Folger MSS Z.e.8, Z.c.36 (113), 449.2;

P.R.O., Requests 2/457, 2/458; *Cal.* 217; H. P. II.41; *Quyny* 27–28, 50, 54–56; *Stratford* 39–40; *MA* IV.39, 62–63, 89; Fripp II.764, 796, 811, 872–76, 890.

17 Council Book A; Warwick Castle MS 2663; MD i.135, 140, iv.71, 72, 198, v.170, xii.54, 71, 119; Wheler MSS i.43; Prerogative Court of Canterbury, 66 Stafforde; Malone II.87, 568, 604; Hunter, *New Illustrations of Shakespeare,* I.52; *Cal.* 63, 167, 226, 248–49, 461; Waters I.615–16; *Quyny* 102, 128, 152, 159–61; *MA* III.148–49; Chambers 3, 112, 172–74; *Wills* I.31–33, II.10–14, 41–43; Fripp I.198, 419, II.792.

18 KB29/228, 29/237; Warwick Castle MS. 2663; MD i.106, iii.31, v.161, vii.141, 142, 145, 149, x.22, xii.62; Fines, 1602, 1604, 1619; Council Book B; H. P., *New Place,* 74–78; H. P. II.91–100; British Record Soc., XXXIX.135; *MA* IV.154–55; Fripp II.620, 798–99, 828, 886. For the name compare Julins Palmer of Coventry (*DNB*), July or Julines Bradshaw of Worcester, who married at Stratford, and the sixteenth-century play *July and Julian* (ed. Giles Dawson, Malone Soc., 1955).

19 Harleian Soc. XXI.69; *Middle Temple Records,* I.357, 426; *Quyny* 154–56, 173–96; Chambers 149–52; Fripp I.167–68, 245, II.543–48, 578; Rupert Taylor in *PMLA,* LX (1945), 81–94. Fripp confused Greene with a recusant of Tanworth (Catholic Record Soc. XVIII.344, 347) and with a yeoman of Broad Marston mentioned by Sturley ("Thomas Greenes band of Marston").

20 MD viii.174; Ingleby 4; *Middle Temple Records,* II.611; *Short-Title Catalogue,* nos. 21,297–99; *Stratford* 59–60; *The Works of Michael Drayton,* ed. Hebel, Tillotson, and Newdigate, V (1941), xxiii–iv, 66; Newdigate, *Michael Drayton and His Circle,* 200; F. B. Williams, Jr., *Index of Dedications* (to be published by the Bibliographical Society).

21 Council Book B; MD i.1, 2, v.92, vii.125–29, viii.1, x.23, xi.1, xiii.42; *Cal.* 216–17, 354; Chambers 105, 126, 151–52; Fripp II.631, 762–64, 805–12, 833–37, 898–99; *VHW* III.250.

22 Council Book B; Throckmorton MSS at Birthplace; MD viii.1, xvi.27; *Cal.* 225, 463; H. P. II.36–41; Chambers 143, 152, 164; Fripp II.731–32, 764, 797, 800, 834, 890, 897.

CHAPTER IX

1   Chambers 90–95, 142–43, 153–59.
2   MD i.4, vii.125, xii.103; *Cal.* 354; Halliwell[-Phillipps], *Extracts from the Vestry-Book* (1865), 88; Wellstood, nos. 47, 60; Chambers 96, 151–53; Fripp II.670, 725, 762–63.
3   Council Book B; H. P. (1848), 105.
4   MD i.4; H. P. (1848), 104; H. P., *Shakespearian Facsimiles* (1863); H. P. I.377–93; Richard Savage in *Athenaeum,* Aug. 29, 1908.
5   Accounts; Council Book B; MD v.221a, xi.3, xvi.21; Wheler MSS i.79–81; Prerogative Court of Canterbury, 101 Weldon; H. P., *New Place,* 35; *Contemps.* 236–38; *Stratford* 56–57; Chambers 142; Fripp II.702, 787, 801–2, 838–45.
6   Accounts; Council Book B; H. P. (1848), 105–6, 270; H. P., *New Place,* 26–27; Chambers 153; Fripp II.789, 893.
7   Thomas Beard, *The Theatre of Gods Judgements* (1597, 1612), 197; Lewis Bayly, *The Practise of Pietie* (12th edn., 1620), 432; MD i.164, vii.106, 120, 122, xvi.14; Wheler MSS i.65, 70; R. B. Wheler, *History of Stratford-upon-Avon* (1806), 15.
8   Council Book B; Wheler MSS i.64–68, 109; MD i.94, vii.17, xiii.8, 11, 27–29; Ingleby; H. P. I.22, 247–51, II.36–39; *Envir.* 81–91; Chambers 141–52; Lewis II.451–67; *VHW* III.267–68. The vicar of Mickleton near Stratford opposed enclosure in 1616: W. B. Willcox, *Gloucestershire* (1940), 280–82.
9   MD i.107, 108, v.18, 151–62, vii.1–27, viii.2, 175, xiii.5–13, 27–29; Council Book B; Wheler MSS i.67–85; Ingleby; Chambers 143–52; Lewis II.458–66; *VHW* III.267–68.
10 MD xiii.23; R. E. Brettle in *Modern Language Review,* XXII (1927), 7–14; *MA* IV.62, 117; *VHW* III.101.
11 P.R.O., Star Chamber 8/26/10; Gray 67, 134, 248; Chambers 7–8; Hotson, *I, William Shakespeare,* 275, 287; Fripp II.824, 839–42.
12 Accounts; MD v.153; Malone II.629; *Cal.* 125–26; H. P. I.169, 254–57, 272–73, II.305–7; Fripp II.763, 821, 832–33, 887–88, 903–7.
13 Chambers 169–80; Lewis II.471–83. William Palmer of Leamington, Gloucs., left "unto Elizabeth my wief all hir wearing apparell

and my second best fetherbed for hir selfe furnished, And one other meaner fetherbed furnished for hir mayde," besides doubling the income he had settled on her when they married, "in Consideracion that she is a gentlewoman and drawing towardes yeres, And that I wolde have hir to live as one that were and had bien my wief" (will of 1573, Prerogative Court of Canterbury, 38 Peter).

14 Court; MD v.93, 188; H. P. (1848), 234-40; *Cal.* 211, 231, 242, 460; H. P. I.242, II.53; Chambers, *William Shakespeare,* I.505-7, II.169-80; *Wills* I.4-5.

15 MD xiii.97; H. P. (1848), 30; *Cal.* 463-64; H. P. I.387-94, II.62-63, 117-18; Chambers 4-13, 34; Bentley, *The Jacobean and Caroline Stage,* II.463-64.

16 Accounts for 1608, 6s. to players; H. P. (1848), 239; H. P. II.13; Parish Register Soc. LIII.11, 19, 164; *Stratford* 36; Fripp II.904-8.

17 Folger MS 2073.5, printed in *Diary of the Rev. John Ward,* ed. Severn (1839), 183; Chambers, *William Shakespeare,* I.86, 89, II.249-50, 257; Lewis II.526.

18 Chambers 182-85, 240-41; Katharine Esdaile in *Essays and Studies, 1952* (English Association), 26-31.

INDEX

Abington, 143
Acton, Joyce, 74
Acton, schoolmaster, 55
Acton, Middlesex, 111
Addenbrooke, John, 107, 110
Aesop, 38
Aglionby, Edward, 79–80
Ainge. *See* Ange
Alcester, 6, 76, 107
Alderminster, 116, 117, 130
Alen, schoolmaster, 54
Aleppo, 62
Alvechurch, 102
Alveston, 30, 50, 116
Alwin, sheriff of Warwick, 12
Anderson, Sir Edmund, 98
Ange, Arthur, 142
Ange, Edward, 116
Ange (Ainge), George, 41
Ange (Ainge), George, jr., 41
Ange (Ainge), John, 39, 41
Ange, Richard, 10, 42
ap Williams, Joan, 47
ap Williams, Lewis, 46–47
ap Williams, Lewis, jr., 47
Archer, Andrew, 137
Arden, Agnes (wife of Robert), 16–18,
    19, 20, 21, 64, 103
Arden, Agnes (daughter of Robert).
    See Stringer
Arden, Alice (wife of William), 14
Arden, Alice (daughter of Robert), 17,
    18, 22, 30
Arden, Christopher, 16
Arden, Edward, 12, 75, 79

Arden, Eleanor, 13, 15
Arden, Elizabeth (daughter of Robert).
    See Scarlett
Arden, Elizabeth (1588), 16
Arden, Geoffrey, 12
Arden, Geoffrey (of Coventry), 14
Arden, Sir Henry, 12
Arden, Henry, 13, 14
Arden, Joan. *See* Lambert
Arden, John (son of Robert), 13
Arden, John (of Long Itchington), 14
Arden, John (of Marton), 14
Arden, Sir John, 13, 14, 15
Arden, Joyce, 17, 22, 30
Arden, Katherine. *See* Edkins
Arden, Margaret. *See* Webbe
Arden, Martin, 13
Arden, Mary. *See* Shakespeare
Arden, Sir Ralph, 12
Arden, Richard, 14
Arden, Robert (d. 1452), 12–13
Arden, Robert (of Lapworth), 14
Arden, Robert (of Snitterfield), 12,
    14–15
Arden, Robert (of the court), 13–14
Arden, Robert (of Wilmcote), 9, 12,
    14, 15–18, 20, 22, 23, 25, 30, 63,
    84, 85, 86, 142
Arden, Robert (d. 1636), 12
Arden, Simon, 86
Arden, Thomas (son of Robert), 13,
    14
Arden, Thomas (son of Walter), 13
Arden, Thomas (son of Sir John), 13,
    86

172